# THE BUSINESS SPEECH:

## Speaker, Audience, and Text

**James VanOosting**
*Southern Illinois University*

Prentice-Hall, Inc., Englewood Cliffs, N.J. 07632

**Library of Congress Cataloging in Publication Data**

VanOosting, James.
  The business speech.

  Includes bibliographies and index.
  1. Public speaking.  2. Communication in management.
I. Title.
PN4193.B8V36  1984        808.5′1′08865        84-4811
ISBN 0-13-107830-5

Editorial/production supervision: Pam Price
Interior design: Richard C. Laveglia
Cover design: Mark Berghash, 20/20 Services, Inc.
Manufacturing buyer: Ed O'Dougherty

To
**Wallace Bacon**
**Allen Goetcheus**
**Lilla Heston**
**Jessica Rousselow**

**who taught me to hear the human voice**

Printed in the United States of America

10  9  8  7  6  5  4  3  2  1

ISBN 0-13-107830-5    01

Prentice-Hall International, Inc., *London*
Prentice-Hall of Australia Pty. Limited, *Sydney*
Editora Prentice-Hall do Brasil, Ltda., *Rio de Janeiro*
Prentice-Hall Canada Inc., *Toronto*
Prentice-Hall of India Private Limited, *New Delhi*
Prentice-Hall of Japan, Inc., *Tokyo*
Prentice-Hall of Southeast Asia Pte. Ltd., *Singapore*
Whitehall Books Limited, *Wellington, New Zealand*

# Contents

# Preface

This study investigates the composition, delivery, and perception of business speeches. Public speaking is but one of several communication skills required of persons in business. Other necessary abilities include letter and report writing, interviewing, small group participation, modes of leadership, media management, and interpersonal relations within an organization. Whereas many textbooks in the area of business communication introduce each of these subjects and include public speaking as a list item, our attention is devoted entirely to the live communication of one-to-many—public speaking. *The Business Speech: Speaker, Audience, and Text* is offered as an introduction to the subject for college and university students. It may serve, too, as a workshop guide to business professionals.

In selecting and organizing materials for the book, I have made two assumptions about its reader. First, the reader has completed successfully a basic course in composition or speech. Thus, I do not include, for instance, a grammatical review. Second, the reader is making this study concurrent with the study of basic business subjects. Thus, I restrict the book's focus to aspects of communication and do not attempt a general introduction to business terms or ideas.

*The Business Speech* is divided into two parts. Chapters 1–14 consider the communication principles that govern public speaking in a business setting. While these discussions aim at a pragmatic explanation of speech making and its problems, they are deliberately philosophical. Chapters 15–22 are decidedly practical in their structure and intent. Each one offers guidance and practice in the composition, delivery, and perception of a particular kind of business speech. My decision to construct the book in this way reflects a conviction that good communication practice must be grounded in a knowledge of basic principles. Hence, theory precedes application. The plan is also based upon a desire that the book's second part should serve as a convenient source of reference.

While the organization of any textbook prescribes, to some extent, its proper use in a classroom, I have tried to avoid dictating a course structure. Chapters 1–14 interconnect in a logical and necessary sequence. Chapters 15–22 proceed, by arbitrary choice, in an order determined by textual complexity—from a speech of introduction to the verbal report. One instructor may be comfortable with dividing the course outline in conjunction with my chapter divisions; another may prefer interspersing chapters from the second half of the book with discussions in the first part.

In addition to the four people named in the dedication, I express public thanks for their help and encouragement to members of the Department of Speech Communication at Southern Illinois University, especially to Marion Kleinau and Ron Pelias. I thank my colleagues Don MacDonald and Mary Lou Higgerson for permission to include the sample speech transcripts in Chapters 7 and 8 respectively. For her research assistance with the sample speeches in Chapters 20 and 21, I thank Lori Schmidt.

# I

# PRINCIPLES OF BUSINESS SPEAKING

# 1

# At the Outset

To make a separate study of business speech is to define the experience as somehow distinct from other public speaking situations, and to see it as unique among other forms of business communication. Both assumptions could be argued. "Business speech" is a generic label covering a range of settings, subjects, audiences, and speakers. Each business speech, while individual and peculiar in its way, bears a resemblance to all other oratory—political, religious, didactic, and even comedic. When studying a business speech, thus, general principles of public communication apply. Nevertheless, the purposes and practices of business speaking mark it as a distinct experience worthy of special study. Furthermore, while business speaking and commercial writing have much in common, they are enough unlike to warrant separate consideration.

*The Business Speech: Speaker, Audience, and Text* addresses its subject with a practical purpose, with an orientation to the business professional, and with two biases: (1) that good public communication rarely happens by accident, and (2) that it can be made to happen by design. What may seem at the outset to be a narrow topic—the business speech—actually contains myriad complexities that are often hidden to the casual observer, disguised by the workaday familiarity of most business speech settings. This study allows us to focus a special spotlight on the mundane and to probe its features for what may be extraordinary. An assumption throughout is that the business speech is, basically, an experience of human communication—important, multidimensional, capable of causing change, with a creative potential both productive and dangerous.

## WHAT IS A BUSINESS SPEECH?

The term "business speech" evokes a number of conventional images: a salesperson extolling the advantages of a new product line, the advertising executive displaying a promotional campaign, the market analyst charting a financial forecast, or the industrial manager urging workers to meet higher standards of quality or efficiency. All these situations describe business speech activities. However, business speaking includes many other situations that may not come to mind as readily. This broader range may be illustrated by contrasting the settings and purposes of in-house meetings and public forums, of an audience of consumer advocates and an annual gathering of shareholders, of a hands-on training program and a formal scientific convention, of an entertaining acceptance speech and a highly technical verbal report. Our working definition of a "business speech" must cover all these settings.

Does the definition of business speech include a situation in which

a corporate executive is invited to speak at a high school's career day or to lecture in the college classroom?
an economic forecaster gives an opinion of the grain futures market on a local TV program?
a company official is asked to defend air quality controls at a town meeting?
a bank president steps before the microphones to explain his or her sudden resignation?
an auto company executive testifies before a congressional committee to advocate foreign import quotas?
a plant union representative asks for a strike vote from the membership?
a shareholder makes a proposal at an annual meeting?

All these situations and more could be included under the general heading of "business speech." Yet, dramatic differences exist among the examples cited. Part of the task of this study is to consider underlying principles of public communication without generalizing unfairly about disparate types of speech situations.

As a working definition of "business speech," we may include

1. any public speech given by a person in business when he or she is representing a corporate interest,
2. any public speech of which the primary subject is related to business concerns,
3. any public speech for which the primary audience is composed of business personnel, or
4. any public speech aimed primarily at achieving a commercial end.

As our discussion evolves, each of these qualifications must be tested against individual case studies. At the outset, it is important to note that "business speech" cannot be defined solely on the basis of a speaker's identity, the subject of a speech text, the profile of an audience, or the persuasive intent of a given speech event. Each of these components is integral to public communication, and we are interested primarily in how they work together—how they influence one another.

## SPEAKER, AUDIENCE, AND TEXT

This book's subtitle indicates a certain approach to the speech process. Speaker, audience, and text are integrally linked in a communication event; an understanding of one component without due consideration of the other two can yield only a partial, distorted understanding of the whole event. Any real communication that takes place in a business speech is the result of merged interests and perceptions on the parts of speaker and listener; the contract guaranteeing that merger is a speech's text, its language and logic.

The communication event of a business speech begins with the speaker, with his or her presence, identity, bearing, and voice. Everything that a speaker is and does contributes to, or detracts from, communication—the speaker's appearance, dress, physical stature, movement, gesture, mannerisms, tone, inflection, and characteristic attitude. Unless a business speaker is properly trained, these aspects of performance can make their impact without his or her knowledge and outside the individual's control. Likewise, a naïve member of the audience may make judgments and determine meanings on the basis of these unconscious performance behaviors. We shall devote considerable attention to the speaker's oratorical skills because they can enhance or undermine the persuasive impact of a speech. But no speaker, however skillful, is totally in charge of communication.

To understand the complexity (and fragility) of a speech event, one must also appreciate the role of audience perception. The truism that one gets out of an experience in kind what one puts in applies in many ways to the audience of a business speech. The ultimate test of effective speech must be measured by audience response—the levels of understanding and commitment *after* hearing a speech contrasted to *prior* knowledge and attitudes. These changes depend as much upon a listener's skills, interests, and aptitudes as they do upon a speaker's ability. We must look closely, then, at the place and function of audience perception in business speech so that we may improve our effectiveness as listeners *and* as speakers.

Whereas every detail of the public speaking situation—from a speaker's toothy grin to a listener's hard seat—plays its part in communication, most important is the speech's text, *what* is said. A speech text, even that of a simple demonstration, is complex. It contains a speaker's ideas, reflects a certain logic (or lack of logic), and uses a specific vocabulary, which itself indicates many things. A speech text says much about a speaker's knowledge of a given subject and reveals his or her authority to address the issue. The words and structure of a text can indicate, as well, a speaker's attitude toward, and feelings about, an audience. We shall see that a speech text, when examined closely, projects a miniature replica of the whole public speaking event.

This study of the business speech, thus, examines a multilayered experience, a communication event. We shall separate its dimensions for the sake of analysis, looking individually at the speaker, the audience, and the text. But our thinking will always return to the interaction among these three components because it is this dynamic relationship that really describes speech communication. We are interested in the interplay among language, speaker, and listener—with the common links among composition, performance, and perception.

## APPROACH: THEORY AND PRACTICE

The matched objectives of this textbook are (1) to improve the public speaking ability of business professionals, and (2) to increase the capacity for accurate perception on the part of speech audiences. Both aims are ambitious; they require rigorous study and application. To meet these objectives, the book moves constantly between theory and practice, philosophy and experience. If, by term's end, a student has developed certain skills as an orator but lacks a philosophical understanding of those skills and their communication impact, our aims will not have been met. Likewise, if an individual becomes conversant in theoretical issues of public communication but cannot apply these to specific business situations, his or her knowledge will have limited value. Our approach to learning, thus, demands both thinking and doing with a special regard for the intimate connections between theory and practice.

Several aids to this dual learning approach have been incorporated into the book's structure. First, the text as a whole is divided into two parts. The first, longer section considers underlying principles of business speaking, while the second part gives attention to the practice of business speaking in specific situations. Yet, these formal divisions do not separate theory and practice; various means have been devised to assure the dual approach throughout.

Beginning with Chapter 2, each chapter starts off by stating its subject, defining necessary terms, and discussing certain principles of communication. Learning then moves from theory to practice with a series of exercises designed to apply those principles discussed in the introductory essay. Following the exercise section is a sample speech with discussion of its merits and problems. At the end of each chapter, the student is presented with a hypothetical business assignment and is asked to respond by creating an appropriate speech.

The movement between theory and practice within each chapter, which is also implicit in the book's overall structure, underscores our pragmatic aims. This is *not* a book of theory; it *is* a laboratory experience in public speaking for the business professional and aspirant. But the experiments conducted in this laboratory must be informed by a solid understanding of basic principles. Nowhere more than in today's business enterprise do the theory and practice of speech communication merge. If business speech practices do not reflect sensible theory, their communication results cannot be reliable. Furthermore, if business speech practices do not contribute to our general understanding of human communication, something is seriously wrong. Sensible theory and studied practice are inseparable components of the successful business speaker's training.

## A PREVIEW

Part I, "Principles of Business Speaking," is divided into four sections, each comprised of three chapters. Chapters 2–4 look at the business *speaker*—his or her identity and context, intention and credibility, and role as a performer. Chapters 5–7 shift focus to the speech *audience* with discussions of analysis and projection, the skills of listening and viewing, and the functions of assessment and response. In Chapters 8–10, the idea of a *text* is examined—topic selection and research, information exchange, and strategies of persuasion. Three areas of special consideration receive attention in Chapters 11–13: directing a convention, ghost writing, and the speech in print. Part I concludes in Chapter 14 with a philosophical overview.

Part II, "The Practice of Business Speaking," looks at eight specific speech types, from a simple introduction to the more complicated situations of a motivational speech and a verbal report. In each instance, the speech type is defined and illustrated with a discussion of the special features and responsibilities of the speaker, the audience and the text. As with the chapters in Part I, these latter chapters offer hypothetical cases for student speeches. Following Part II is an Appendix that outlines strategies for continued study.

As suggested in the preface, chapters from the second part of the book may be interspersed with those from Part I, or topics for study may proceed in sequence from Chapters 2 through 22. In either case, a student is expected to follow closely the interplay between idea and experience.

## SUMMARY

Business speaking is a division that falls under the larger heading of public communication. It deserves special attention as a separate subject because of its distinctive purposes and practices within a commercial culture. Our study is designed for the business professional and apprentice. Its two aims are pragmatic: to improve a student's public speaking ability and to increase the skills of perception in a business audience.

For the purposes of this study, business speaking is defined to include (1) any public speech given by a person in business when he or she is representing a corporate interest, (2) any public speech in which the primary subject is related to business concerns, (3) any public speech for which the primary audience is composed of business personnel, or (4) any public speech aimed primarily at achieving a commercial end.

Any accurate description of a business speech event must take into account the roles of speaker, audience, and text. Each variable contributes to meaning. As students and practitioners of business speaking, we are interested especially in the interplay among these components—how they affect one another. Our study, while designed with a practical thrust and a professional orientation, is as much concerned with underlying principles of communication as with the behavioral signs of speech performance. Sensible theory and effective practice cannot be separated.

In the chapters to come, we shall consider a business speech event from the separate perspectives of speaker, audience, and text. Binding the whole together is a constant concern with meaning, both as intended by a speaker and as perceived by an audience. And underpinning this textbook from start to finish is a conviction that all business communication, including public speaking, is human communication—personal and worldly, essential to individual and corporate welfare.

# 2

# The Speaker: Identity and Context

A serious study of public speaking could begin at any of several points, so rich and diverse is the communication event. A careful observer might start by surveying the physical setting in which a speech occurs, or by analyzing the human environment and the audience's expectations of the speech event. One could begin by profiling the vested interests of all participants, speaker and listeners, and the influence upon communication of corporate loyalties and viewpoints. The investigation of a given speech might begin with the close scrutiny of a printed transcript. Where one's consideration of public speaking begins is not nearly so important as where it ends. One can begin anywhere, with anything, but a reliable understanding of the experience as a whole demands pursuing all lines of inquiry and their points of connection with one another. Our study begins with a close look at the business *speaker* and, especially in this chapter, with some understanding of that speaker's identity and context.

## WHO IS THE BUSINESS SPEAKER?

To begin, this question cannot be answered in the singular: there is no such thing as *the* business speaker. There are only business speakers in the plural, and the distinction implies an interesting starting point for discussion. Very few commercial enterprises employ professional speakers *per se*, individuals whose job descriptions begin and end with speech. There are company spokespersons, of course, specialists in corporate communication, and (occasionally) full-time speech writers. However, by far the largest number of business speaking situations call upon the skills of amateurs—executives, managers, and other personnel trained in nonspeech areas. These individuals hold their authority by virtue of many different skills, including good decision making, technical expertise of various kinds, effective personnel management, ability in sales, or financial acumen. The discipline and discernment required for success in any business area should serve the speaker well, but these other skills alone cannot guarantee success in speaking. The individual whose job requires occasional public communication must develop competencies unique to that assignment. For the person in business, these speech skills usually must be acquired in addition to other professional training. The first thing that can be said about the business speaker, then, is that he or she is probably an amateur on the podium and in need of special training.

Whether or not one enjoys public speaking or has a "knack" for it, very few business managers or executives can avoid the assignment. Speechmaking is integral to the business enterprise. Information must be conveyed; personnel must be motivated and directed; reports must be given; policies must be articulated and defended; meetings must be chaired; products and services must be sold. Usually, a business speaker prepares his message in advance, has an opportunity to practice its delivery, and makes whatever arrangements are necessary to ensure good communication with an audience. However, other occasions demand impromptu speaking, as when an individual is called upon at a meeting to explain a decision or to defend a proposal. Whether one gets up in front of a public gathering to introduce the company president or addresses a small sales staff the first thing each morning, one is engaged in public communication, making speeches. So a second thing that must be said about the business speaker is that public communication is his or her workaday expectation and not some extraordinary assignment reserved for special occasions.

The purposes of business speech range widely: to sell, to teach, to interest, to defend, to apologize, to cajole, to amuse, to confront, to encourage, to negotiate, to calm, to arouse; there are as many variations on the human voice and intention as there are speakers and situations demanding speech. Common to *all* business speaking situations, however, is their commercial context. That is, any business speech will be understood partly by its perceived relationship to specific corporate objectives. The business speaker is seen and heard by others as a representative of a company, a service, a product, a management team, a union, a consumer group, or some other specific constituency. Whether or not this association between speaker and business context is intended or accurate, it is a variable of communication that must be acknowledged and dealt with. This, then, is the third feature in our initial profile of the business speaker: he or she is viewed as representing some larger business interest. A business speaker may be described as an amateur in public communication, as one whose job frequently requires speech skills, and as a representative of some larger business interest.

## JOB DESCRIPTION

Trading one's amateur status for some level of speech mastery begins with a business speaker understanding his or her general job description. When making a speech, regardless of the situation or the objective, a person in business has three responsibilities. More accurately, one may be held accountable by three overseers: the subject, the audience, and the business constituency that one represents.

Any public speaker's first obligation is the fair and thorough treatment of a topic. Unless one has "done right" by a subject, treated it with serious respect, all other components of the speech process are voided. Meeting one's responsibility to a subject involves careful research, precise definition, logical thinking, objective judgment, and a straight appraisal of one's own limitations. The following questions represent a minimal test of a speaker's responsibility to a subject:

1. Has the speaker gathered all available information relevant to a topic?
2. Are his or her resources current and reliable?
3. Are the research methods used valid, verifiable, and accurate in their recording?
4. Does a speaker possess the necessary background information to assess all dimensions of a topic?
5. Does he or she understand the specialized vocabulary associated with the topic?

We shall return often to the speaker's accountability to a subject. Suffice it here to state that a business speaker is responsible for the accuracy, completeness, and validity of everything that he or she says about a given subject. In some instances, this reponsibility carries with it the weight of legal sanction; in all instances, an audience depends upon a speaker's authority to address sensibly a speech topic.

In many ways, a speaker's obligations to subject matter overlap his or her accountability to the listener. A speaker, perhaps even more than a writer, must be held accountable by an audience. At least with compostion, the reader has a printed text to verify perceptions and to hold the writer to his or her word. The acoustic experience of speech is more ephemeral than print, more elusive. A listener cannot double check a reference in a speech or reread difficult portions, as one can with a book. Thus, the speaker bears a great responsibility to get it right the first time, to make a message clear to an audience without the aid of a glossary or footnotes. The business speaker's general responsibilities to a listener may be tested by the following questions:

1. Does the speaker arrest and hold attention from the beginning to the end of the speech?
2. Does the speaker's pattern of organization allow a listener to follow changing topics with ease?
3. Are all outside references and authorities noted clearly, with sufficient information for the listener to verify them?
4. Is all information necessary for the audience's fair judgment included in the speech?
5. Does the speaker present material in a compelling way so that it can be remembered accurately?

It is not sufficient that the speaker alone understand a topic. Communication dividends are only paid on the basis of a listener's comprehension after a speech, and the speaker is accountable to that listener just as a corporate official is accountable to shareholders.

A third responsibility is implied in the business speaker's job description, an obligation to a specific constituency. In almost every business speech situation, the speaker is viewed by an audience as representing some larger interest or group: a company, a union, a department, a political action committee, or some other advocacy group. Whether or not the speaker acknowledges this corporate voice or uses the plural "we," representation is assumed. Hence, a speaker may rightly be held accountable by the unnamed others whose viewpoint he or she represents. The fulfillment of this responsibility may be measured by answering these questions:

1. Does a speaker identify clearly the group and viewpoint that he or she represents?
2. Is the extent of agreement within a group represented accurately?
3. Are disagreements or minority reports within a group acknowledged and represented fairly?
4. Does the speaker differentiate clearly when he or she is speaking for the group and when not?
5. Does the speech's content, structure, and style project a fair picture of the group's attitude toward, and degree of commitment to, a topic?

Much more must be said about a business speaker's role as corporate representative because group identity has a significant impact upon individual credibility.

At first thought, the idea of public speaking may be associated with highly personal and individualistic images—one person getting up in front of a crowd and offering his or her opinions. In fact, a mature speaker accepts responsibility for understanding many perspectives other than his or her own. The job description of an effective business speaker demands strict accountability to a given subject, to a given audience, and to a given constituency. Each area requires specific tasks and attitudes of the speaker, and the achievement of each task requires specific skills.

## PUBLIC RELATIONS

Underlying this introductory description of a business speaker is the issue of public relations. Not all speeches are given by PR specialists, nor do all speeches have as their primary objective the building of a public image. Nevertheless, every business speech, regardless of purpose or context, has a public relations function. Every speech seeks to enhance the public perception of its speaker, its viewpoint, or its implied constituency.

Public relations is a topic we will return to frequently in our discussion; it is a term that must be defined with care early on. One popular conception of the public relations objective is that of creating a public image of a person, a product, or a company—an image that may or may not describe the fact. This idea of public relations enjoys wide acceptance and is nourished by myths of the greedy politician who projects an image of altruism or the corporate conglomerate portrayed as a modest mom-and-pop operation. In these extreme cases, it is the public relations expert who is seen as perpetrating the lie, masquerading the truth behind a clever disguise.

Our use of the term *public relations* does not carry with it this negative connotation, though these associations must be acknowledged. Public relations is not a matter of creating an image to *disguise* the truth; it is planning a strategy of communication to *reveal* the truth. The need for public relations specialists in business, and the need to consider a public relations dimension to every business speech, indicate the difficulty of accurate public perception. What the PR expert reminds all public speakers is that stating only the facts about a given situation or speaking only the truth about a set of circumstances may not be sufficient to convince an audience of those facts or that truth. Reliable, persuasive public communication requires a strategy of presentation that compels attention and wins trust.

Speaking to a group of any size is, by definition, an act of public communication, and any astute business person is concerned about relations with that public. In later chapers devoted to the idea of an audience, we shall discuss different publics and different categories of public interest. We want to make it clear from the outset that a public relations dimension is integral to every business speaking situation and to begin thinking about the implications of that simple statement.

The public nature of speech situations places certain constraints on communication, as well as affording unique opportunities. In dealing with public perception, there can be no private agreements or understandings, no secret handshakes or codes, no club names or jargon. Public communication, if it is to succeed, must establish an open, accessible relationship between speaker and audience. And the foundation of that public relationship depends for its strength upon the speech skills of business professionals at every level of a corporate enterprise.

## EXERCISES

**A**   As a beginning exercise, test your own preconceptions of business speech by answering the following questions. Write down whatever comes first to mind; there are no right or wrong answers. After each student has filled in the questionnaire, draw a composite profile of preconceptions held by the class.

1. What level of a business organization do most speakers represent (e.g., top executive, middle management, staff)?

2. Is the typical audience for most business speeches comprised of the speaker's peers, subordinates, superiors, or other groups?

3. Is the typical business speech memorized, delivered from notes or outline, read from a manuscript, or does it follow some other approach?

4. When a business executive appears on television to represent a corporate position, what are the likely first impressions of a consumer-viewer?

5. What is the typical length, in minutes, of a promotional speech delivered at a sales convention?

6. What percentage of business speeches are delivered by women?

7. Does the typical business speech employ visual aids? If so, what aids are used most often?

8. Rank in order from most to least important the aims of a typical business speech.

   to entertain          _____
   to sell               _____
   to inform             _____
   to train              _____
   to defend             _____
   to apologize          _____

9. Characterize the kind and quality of humor used in a business speech.

10. Rank the following professions in terms of speaker credibility. That is, if you were to hear a speech by a representative of each profession, which speaker would you think most reliable and trustworthy? Place a *1* by the most credible, and so on, through *10* for the least.

| | |
|---|---|
| minister, rabbi, priest | _____ |
| attorney | _____ |
| member of Congress | _____ |
| corporate executive | _____ |
| professor | _____ |
| doctor | _____ |
| consumer advocate | _____ |
| sales manager | _____ |
| city council member | _____ |
| architect | _____ |

**B**  List as many types of business speech as you can envision (e.g., a chairperson's address to the annual meeting of shareholders or a supervisor's policy announcement to department personnel). To construct a comprehensive list, it may help to change roles within a business organization. That is, put yourself alternately in the place of a top executive, a manager, a staff member, an industrial worker, a shareholder, and so on. Imagine the kinds of speeches that you would likely make or listen to as part of each job. Then compile the individual lists into a class list.

1. _____
2. _____
3. _____
4. _____
5. _____
6. _____
7. _____
8. _____
9. _____
10. _____
11. _____
12. _____
13. _____
14. _____
15. _____

**C**  Compile a list of adjectives that should characterize an *ideal* business speech:

1. _____
2. _____
3. _____
4. _____
5. _____
6. _____
7. _____

8. _____

9. _____

10. _____

Identify an individual in public life (whether in business, politics, religion, entertainment, or some other profession) who seems to you to be an expert speaker. In a concise paragraph, defend your choice with specific reasons.

**D** In a brief essay, explain what you take to be three essential differences between *verbal* and *written* communication.

## SAMPLE SPEECH

Read the following speech transcript. It records verbatim the announcement made to all personnel in assembly at the Peterson Production Company, a manufacturer of small machine parts employing approximately 150 workers. This short speech was made at a Friday afternoon meeting in the company's warehouse, the only space large enough to accommodate the audience. (The meeting itself had been announced over the intercom just fifteen minutes before its scheduled time to begin.) There was only one speaker on the agenda, Frank Long, assistant to the president, and he got up to speak without introduction.

Good afternoon.

I appreciate your attendance at this hastily called meeting. While the meeting may seem hasty, the announcement I've come to make was not arrived at hastily. It reflects careful and long deliberation on the parts of all Peterson executives.

I am instructed to inform you of a decision made with regret by Peterson management, that effective two weeks from today, on August 14, Peterson Production Company will discontinue operations in Cincinnati. The reasons behind this action are simple: we have operated at a loss for two consecutive years and cannot continue to sustain such loss. Peterson management does not foresee a turnaround in this situation and, thus, has decided to close the doors in Cincinnati.

We realize that this difficult corporate decision places each of you in a state of personal hardship. The company regrets this and wishes it could be otherwise. To alleviate undue strain and to facilitate your transition to new jobs, we were eager to make this announcement to you at the earliest possible date.

All Peterson workers will continue to be employed for the next two weeks. On Monday, at 3:00 P.M., we shall ask you to meet back here in the warehouse at which time John Brace, director of personnel, will discuss with you all questions related to final pay period, unemployment benefits and procedures, and employment opportunities elsewhere. He will be happy to answer all questions at that time.

I am afraid that no questions can be taken today.

The importance of this brief speech, taking no more than sixty seconds to deliver, cannot be overestimated. Its formal style, straightforward diction, and impersonal voice all run counter to the enormous personal impact the speech is likely to have on each listener. Unlike many other business speech situations, there was no need here to get or hold audience attention. The gravity of the business context, a plant closure, ensured attention.

This transcript could be analyzed on several levels. We could talk about the organization of information, the level of vocabulary, the selection of detail (what information was included and what was excluded), the brevity, and the corporate voice implied by noun and pronoun references. If we had been at the speech site, or could view a videotape, other dimensions of communication might be discussed: the speaker's tone of voice and bearing, the physical setup of the makeshift auditorium, any signs of status difference between speaker and listeners, and visible cues to audience response. However, we shall limit our discussion, in this case, to the transcript itself and to the speaker's accountabilities.

Did the speaker, Mr. Long, fulfill his responsibilities to the subject? A satisfactory answer to the question would assume some clear idea of what the subject was. If one takes the speech's sole topic to be an announcement of the decision to close, this speaker did the job. If, however, the speech objective was any broader (e.g., to announce an executive decision and to explain its rationale), Mr. Long must be given much lower marks. In fact, the speech offers only weak argument in support of the decision to close; he offers no evidence, explanation, or example. This terse announcement, with its minimum of information, is not likely to win the confidence, much less concurrence, of an audience. To the contrary, the information left out of the speech that might reasonably have been there raises many unanswered questions. Only by a very narrow definition of the speech topic could one say that Mr. Long fulfilled his primary obligation.

A speaker's second accountability, to the audience, is badly neglected in this case. There is little evidence in the transcript to suggest that Mr. Long, or the executives whom he represents, can identify with this audience's knowledge, needs, or feelings. The practical result of this speech is that 150 people will be out of work in two weeks. While the most sensitive speaker could not change that hard fact or alter its impact, any careful speaker should be able to go farther than Mr. Long did in identifying with audience needs and perceptions. This announcement means the radical upheaval of lives and livelihoods, the breaking up of personal and business ties, and an array of pragmatic and psychological problems for the listeners to solve. A good speaker could anticipate the audience's dismay, anger, and bewilderment, addressing these responses directly. At a minimum, the audience deserves more information from the speaker and a much more personal (humane) manner of speech.

If low marks must be given to this speaker for his treatments of subject and audience, somewhat higher marks may be given for his accountability to a constituency. The issue is difficult to decide with certainty on such limited information. Clearly, Mr. Long is a spokesperson for Peterson's executives, specifically for the unnamed president. He announces an executive decision in straightforward language and offers an official explanation of that action. In fact, the whole speech sounds like an impersonal press release. Whether or not Peterson's president and other officers would be pleased with this formal announcement and its probable reception by company employees, the viewpoint of the entire executive echelon is given voice and presence by Mr. Long.

As a whole, this brief speech could not be termed a success. Its lack of consideration for the audience, and its sparse information, are likely to anger and alienate listeners— serious failures in any communication act. While there is no single way to have approached this speech assignment, and there could be no easy way of discharging it, there are certainly many better ways than the approach taken in this example.

## DISCUSSION QUESTIONS

1. If you were a Peterson employee in the audience for this speech, what meaning, if any, would you attach to each of the following observations?
    a. The company president has sent a representative rather than appearing in person.
    b. The announcement is made on a late Friday afternoon.
    c. The meeting was announced over the intercom fifteen minutes ahead of time.
    d. The speaker would answer no questions.

2. What questions about the decision to close the plant does the speech leave unanswered? Are there any ambiguous statements in the speech?

3. Just from the transcript, what prior knowledge would you guess that Peterson employees had about a possible plant closing?

4. Characterize your impression of Peterson's management on the basis of this speech. Be specific, and link your answers to features of the transcript.

5. From the language and structure of this speech, speculate on the speaker's probable tone of voice and manner of delivery. Let several students try an improvised performance of the transcript. How many different voices will the language allow?

6. Discuss alternative approaches to this speech assignment if you were Peterson's president or Mr. Long.

7. What differences would it make to your communication choices if the audience for this speech were Peterson shareholders rather than employees?

## HYPOTHETICAL SPEECH

Imagine that you are a job candidate for the post of director of personnel at a large bank. On the basis of your resumé, references, and a telephone conversation, the bank has flown you in for two days of intensive interviews. At the end of that time, you meet in executive session with the bank's president and five vice-presidents for a two-hour final interview. The first question asked is this:

> As director of personnel, what qualities would you look for in an employee when trying to predict his or her success at a management position?

Give a two-minute impromptu speech answering this question. Remember the situation. You must give a satisfactory answer to the question itself—well organized and specific. At the same time, everything about your delivery and bearing must impress this small audience with your capability as a candidate for a high-level position.

## SUMMARY

Our look at business speech begins with a consideration of the speaker's identity and context. The purposes and occasions of business speech are so many and various that no detailed portrait of the speaker can be drawn. At best, a profile of the typical business speaker may be sketched with three identifying features. First, he or she is professionally competent in other business areas but is probably an amateur speaker in need of specific training in public communication. Second, speaking to variously sized audiences is a frequent and common expectation of the business manager or executive; the assignment is not extraordinary but workaday. Third, a typical business speaker is not perceived by the audience simply as an individual. Beneath and beyond a speaker's single presence may be seen a group interest, a corporate viewpoint, or some commercial end.

A general job description for the business speaker includes three responsibilities, which are separate but interconnected—to treat a subject completely and logically, to address an audience in a clear, memorable way, and to represent accurately a business constituency. For each area of responsibility, the speaker must be held accountable. In a sense, he or she works for three bosses, each with different standards for performance: the subject matter, the audience, and the constituency represented. Despite the hard work and occasional frustration encountered when working for three supervisors, a business speaker dares not ignore one. Effective business communication demands an often delicate merger among separate interests—those of the subject, the audience, and a business constituency—and the speaker serves to negotiate their alliance.

Common to all business speech situations is a concern with good public relations. Because a speaker usually represents some larger group (e.g., a company, a union, shareholders, or consumers), his or her speech must make an accurate impression of that group's viewpoint upon an audience. A successful public relations approach, like a successful speech, does not aim to create a false image but aims to build a representative one—to reveal a speaker's best conception of truth in the most compelling manner.

# 3

# The Speaker: Intention and Credibility

The communication value of a speech can be figured as the sum of a speaker's intentions and a listener's perceptions. Neither alone signifies. Only when speaker and audience have merged their interests and can move in tandem through a speech topic is real communication possible. In this chapter, we shall investigate the whole notion of a speaker's intention and its vital role in effective business speech.

## A SPEAKER'S INTENTION

When faced with any public speaking assignment, one should approach the task as a miniature commercial enterprise and set clear production goals. This analogy is useful in describing a speaker's intention. What he or she hopes to accomplish is not financial profits or stock gains but tangible advances in communication with a particular audience. A speaker's intention refers to the specific communication objectives that he or she expects to meet in a given speech.

Articulating a speaker's intention should be done well in advance of the actual speech event, allowing as much lead time as circumstances permit. It must be admitted at the beginning of this discussion that many business speakers pass over this task or take it for granted, thus destroying any chance of communication success before uttering a single word. Such individuals expect that effective speech is accomplished by instinct, by right of position, or by luck. They approach a speech situation with a vague idea of what might happen, naïvely expecting an audience to fill in any gaps in their own preparation. Such a wishful approach to public communication has precisely the same chance of success as a business enterprise without clear goals—none.

A speaker's intention is like a production goal in three ways. First, both must describe in clear language a high objective worth attaining. No manufacturer sets out to produce at a level of zero-growth; by means of production goals, a company seeks to move forward. Likewise, no speaker should set out to inform an audience of what they already know. The proper aim of public communication is to increase knowledge by giving information, by analyzing data, or by changing perspectives. It is a baffling inconsistency to witness business managers who would never tolerate declines in production who, nevertheless, settle for zero-growth goals in communication. If a speaker's intention is not worth pursuing with a particular audience, if it cannot yield any real profit in communication, then it must be redefined.

Like a production goal, too, a communication objective must be attainable. The first feature of this analogy argued for sufficiently high goals; now the mandate is for goals within reach—not low, but reasonable. A manufacturer may entertain the aim of doubling production in one year, but this remains an idle fantasy unless the necessary materials, personnel, and markets are in place to make the goal attainable. Similarly, the speaker giving a five-minute talk may aim to change an audience's belief about a given issue, but this objective cannot be met unless all circumstances for persuasion are favorable. Deeply held beliefs are not changed quickly; habits are not broken easily; prejudices are not penetrated painlessly. The business speaker aiming to change an audience's attitude or behavior in any way must calculate the resistance and set attainable goals for communication within a given speech.

A third similarity between a speaker's intention and a production goal is that both should be measurable. A goal serves no purpose unless it can mark accomplishment or failure. Manufacturing goals can be measured in terms of units produced, profits realized, labor efficiency, and market shares. Communication goals are less easily monitored and, in some cases, cannot be monitored at all. Some devices for measuring communication effectiveness yield numerical results (e.g., polls, questionnaires, or orders received as the direct result of a speech or sales convention). Other signs of communication success are more subtle and require fine attention on the part of a speaker. A whole range of audience responses during a speech (e.g., movement, yawning, whispering, laughter, and facial expressions) tell the astute speaker something of his or her success.

Speechmaking cannot begin in earnest until the speaker has stated an intention to himself or herself in unequivocal language. That intention must be worthwhile to the audience, reasonable, and measurable. Its statement should be focused sharply, pointing the way along a clear path of discourse. At the beginning, even before the interests of an audience are studied closely, a speaker should ask three questions of himself or herself:

1. What is my primary *subject*?
2. What reasonable *limitations* must be placed on the subject?
3. What is my *attitude* toward this subject?

Only after a speaker has named a topic, defined its scope, and determined a perspective can a speech begin to take shape. Answering these first questions does not define fully a speech objective, but accurate answers provide a reliable starting point. Many speakers do not get this far: their subject is never identified clearly, or they refuse to restrict the subject within useful boundaries, or it is never clear just where the speaker stands in relation to the topic. Speechmaking begins when the speaker can say with some certainty, "I intend to address this subject, with these qualifications, from this perspective." If a speaker could rely upon audience members sharing his or her experience, knowledge, research and viewpoint, these three questions alone would suffice to define a speaker's intention.

## SELF-AWARENESS AND CREDIBILITY

Complete unanimity never exists between speaker and listener, not even in the case of an in-house speech among colleagues. Differences in knowledge, experience, education, age, status, and other variables create differences in perception. Any speaker makes a serious mistake in assuming an audience's total identification with his or her own viewpoint. What seems perfectly apparent and sensible to the speaker may appear ambiguous or unreasonable from another angle of vision. Because of the many and subtle differences of perspective likely to exist between a speaker and an audience, one needs to temper a speech objective with self-awareness.

Effective communication, whether verbal or written, demands some objectivity from its participants. In the case of a business speech, that objectivity must be supplied first by the speaker's self-awareness and, second, by a text that encourages the free and sensible response of an audience. Objective self-awareness means that a speaker must acknowledge to himself or herself the dimensions of one's own knowledge and expertise, the vested interests of one's business position, and the depth of one's commitment to a given viewpoint. By recognizing the uniqueness of a speaker's perspective, one implicitly recognizes the existence of other viewpoints. And, if the speaker possesses any intellectual modesty, one must also acknowledge the likelihood of blind spots existing from any particular angle of vision, including the speaker's own.

A business speaker, both self-aware and astute, should be able to abandon his or her own viewpoint, if only temporarily, and assume the multiple perspectives of others. This is a critical and difficult skill for public speakers to develop—perspective-taking. Its importance to effective speech cannot be stressed too much. If a speaker can identify accurately his or her own vantage point toward a topic, and if one can see the same issue from other viewpoints as well, the chances of meaningful communication taking place are good.

We shall look more closely at perspective-taking and a speaker's proper acknowledgment of the listener in later chapters devoted to the audience. The point here is to remind the speaker that communication depends as much upon perception as upon intention. It is not enough to know a subject and one's own viewpoint, the speaker must also be able to represent that topic and perspective in a credible way.

Credibility is the measure of a speaker's trustworthiness in the mind of an audience member. While the assigning of a credibility rating is done by each listener, a speaker can do much to ensure high marks. From the moment that a speaker is introduced and stands up to address an audience, each listener or viewer begins asking many questions and searching among the speaker's verbal and visual behavior for answers.

Many of these unspoken questions have to do with credibility:

Does the speaker know what he or she is talking about?
Has the speaker had any first-hand experience with the subject?
Is the speaker telling the truth?
Is he or she quoting the best authorities and the most recent studies?
Is the speaker withholding information or suppressing data?
Does the speaker care about the topic?
Does he or she care about the audience?
What motivates the speaker to address this topic at this time before this audience?
Is there a subtext (a meaning beneath the surface) for this speech?

An audience's assessment of speaker credibility is linked at every point to trust: Can the speaker be believed? Can he or she be trusted to know the subject well, to approach it objectively, to care about both the subject and the audience?

A smart speaker anticipates these questions and works hard to assure affirmative answers through every aspect of his or her speech and delivery. Unless a speaker is self-aware and concerned with the believability of his or her viewpoint in the perception of others, no well-fashioned intention will suffice. A speaker's objective must include the determination to influence perception so that one's subject and perspective will deserve an audience's attention.

Achieving credibility in the minds of an audience is critical to any speaker's success. There are no tricks, short cuts, or easy outs to this task. Listeners are right to be wary of investing belief in just any speaker with supposed credentials. A moderate dose of skepticism is healthy for speech audiences, whether in business, politics, or religion, and a good speaker appreciates an audience's caution. Trust must be won by a speaker's thorough research and preparation, by the strengths of logical argument, by the personal and emotional rationality of a position taken, and by the speaker's own compelling presence.

## PERSONA

Every actor in ancient Greek drama wore a mask called a *persona* to signify his character. The actor's job was to live into that persona, to fill the mask with appropriate behavior, to match himself to the unique features of a given character. Actors understand what many public speakers do not: believability is fundamental to persuasion, and believability depends upon consistency. To the theatre audiences of ancient Greece, the appearance of a mask did not carry our modern connotations of concealment or deceit. A mask *revealed* character and personality; it expressed accurately what was unique and consistent in the person represented. That we get our terms *person* and *personality* from a word for *mask* suggests positive and useful implications.

If an ideal persona were to be constructed for the contemporary business speaker, what qualities would it have? What features would have to be molded into the mask to ensure an audience's belief? Of course, public speakers do not literally wear masks, but they do present themselves as actors for the fair judgment of an audience. A business speaker's credible performance should be characterized by features likely to build trust. Here is a beginning list of seven credit-bearing qualities.

1. A believable speech offers *facts* before interpretation. When facts are presented well, without understatement or exaggeration and with ample verification, the speaker builds a solid foundation for persuasion. However, when interpretation is offered without an adequate basis in fact, speaker credibility declines.
2. A believable speech has a solid *organization*, efficient and clear at every point from introduction to conclusion. This structure allows a step-by-step engagement between speaker and listener and guides their movement along a sensible course. Without a clearly marked path of discourse, or with one that meanders aimlessly, a speaker is likely to lose or confuse the listener and, thereby, lose trust.
3. A believable speech, whenever possible, carries its message in a human and personal *vocabulary*, not in bureaucratic, institutional, or technical jargon. Public speaking is, after all, an instance of human communication that links an individual speaker and listener. The more fully members of an audience feel addressed as persons, the more likely they are to respond with trust. A mechanical vocabulary is more likely to elicit a machinelike response—without feeling or conviction.
4. A believable speech makes an integrated *appeal*, satisfying both intellectual and emotional questions in an audience. Credibility decreases when a speaker addresses only one kind of audience response (intellectual *or* emotional) and ignores the whole person.
5. A believable speaker projects *openness* rather than concealment. As soon as an audience senses that information is being withheld, they are right to withdraw trust from the speaker. Openness does not mean that a speaker must reveal secrets or become intimate with the audience. It does mean that any information necessary for an audience's free and fair response to a speech must be given willingly and readily.
6. A believable speaker is fluent in *delivery*. He or she respects language and uses it well, with conciseness and imagination. If a speaker stumbles over words, cannot articulate clearly, has no sense of a sentence's rhythm, or relies upon clichés, credibility is reduced. Audiences assume, rightly or wrongly, that a well-prepared and knowledgeable speaker should not abuse or trip over the language.
7. A believable speaker addresses all audiences with *consideration*, not flippancy or sarcasm. A speaker's courtesy and respect for the listener are more likely to win trust in return than any sign of abusive or coercive behavior.

You might expand this list of credit-yielding features in business speech. They describe a speaker's persona, a mask worn to reveal (not conceal) his or her knowledge, attitudes, and authority.

It might be argued that a skillful performer could affect these winning characteristics and command the unwitting trust of an audience. The best safeguard against such deception in business speech is the fact that a speaker's credibility depends, as well, upon consistency from one context to another. Credibility is a long-term investment. On some occasion, the false mask will crack and destroy, from that time on, a speaker's credibility. These qualities of trustworthiness cannot be put on and taken off like a halloween mask; they must be grown into and filled out like the persona of an ancient Greek actor.

Effective business speech, thus, begins with a speaker's clear statement of an intention. This includes naming the topic, defining its scope, and describing the speaker's characteristic attitude toward that topic. In addition to outlining specific goals for communication, an effective speaker determines ways to win a listener's trust. Both the speaker and the speech must appear credible to an audience if the communication is to realize any real profits.

## EXERCISES

**A**   Here are four hypothetical speech assignments. After each, answer the questions regarding speaker intention.

**1.** You are a junior associate in an advertising agency. At the end of your first year with the firm, you receive a memorandum from the five senior partners. It reads,

> On Friday, August 10, at 4:00 P.M., please be prepared to make a 20-minute presentation in the executive lounge outlining your achievements and professional growth over the year. This customary review will help us get to know you and your work better, and we look forward to it.

Assume that you receive the memorandum on Monday morning and have five days to prepare this presentation. What are your first thoughts? List specifically what you take to be the meeting's purposes.

From the memo alone, profile your anticipated audience in terms of age, status within the organization, level of interest in you and your career, and other significant variables.

Would you plan a formal or an informal presentation? On what basis would you make this decision?

List the specific feelings, attitudes, thoughts, and images with which you would like your audience to depart the presentation.

By what criteria would you select information to be included and emphasized in the presentation?

**2.** You are the dean of a graduate school of business. You have been invited to speak to an assembly of undergraduate juniors majoring in business administration. Your assignment is to describe to these students the variables at work in a decision whether or not to get an MBA degree. The assembly's format calls for you to give a 15- or 20-minute talk, followed by a 40-minute period for questions and answers.

What specifically do you want your audience to know when they leave this assembly?

There are several possible approaches to this speech assignment. One could compare the advantages and disadvantages of enrolling in an MBA program right after graduation versus seeking a job immediately. One might chronicle the steps of admission into an MBA program or compare and contrast various programs. One could cite salary statistics for MBA graduates or outline the career paths of two hypothetical students. Several other approaches might serve well, each reflecting a slightly different intention.

State your aim in taking on this assignment, and describe briefly your best approach to the speech. Defend your answer by showing how the approach meets your aim.

Suggest specific ways in which your speech could help make the question and answer period most profitable.

**3.** You are the personnel director for a midsized electronics manufacturer. The corporation has decided to switch insurance companies covering employee medical benefits. Your assignment on a given day is to accompany the insurance representative to each department, where he or she will explain the new coverage to employees. Your apparently simple speech assignment is to give a one-minute introduction for the insurance representative.

What do you want the audience to feel and think when they depart this meeting? Be specific.

Describe the range of possible attitudes, thoughts, and feelings brought by an audience to such a meeting.

List the specific ways that your one-minute introduction can help move the audience from their predisposition to a desired response. Or, to put it another way, how can your introduction best set the stage for the speech to follow?

By what specific means could your introduction enhance the insurance representative's credibility with the audience?

**4.** You are the chief operating officer of a large savings and loan institution. The chamber of commerce in your city has invited you to make a 15-minute address regarding government regulation of the banking industry.

The assignment itself provides your topic, government regulation, but it leaves open how the subject will be treated. In narrowing the topic and defining its scope, you must decide what you have to say and what this particular audience needs to know.

What would you predict to be this audience's general attitude toward government regulation of business?

What would you predict to be this audience's general attitude toward savings and loan institutions?

List the possible advantages of government regulation in the banking industry. You may need to segment areas of service and to differentiate between a bank and an S & L.

List the possible disadvantages of government regulation of the banking industry.

On balance, describe your attitude toward governmental regulation of your business.

List any areas of specific conflict between your perspective and the likely majority view of your audience.

In one complete sentence, state a reasonable intention for this speech assignment. Be sure to name the topic, limit its scope, and identify your attitude.

**B**   Answer the following questions and perform the suggested exercises in self-awareness. There are no right or wrong answers. Your object is to respond candidly. After doing the exercises, it may be interesting to compare responses as a class.

1. List ten words or phrases that best describe your upbringing (e.g., urban, rural, middle-class, liberal, religious).

_____

_____

_____

_____

_____

_____

_____

_____

_____

_____

2. In complete sentences, state five goals or ambitions that you have set for yourself in business.

3. In a brief paragraph, no more than five or six sentences, describe how you see yourself ten years from now. What is your job? Where do you live? What do you look like? How do you feel?

4. If you had to trade places with someone else, lead his or her life rather than your own, who would you choose? Give two reasons why you would like to be that person. (You may select from persons present or past, male or female, famous or unknown.)

5. List five words or phrases that describe the qualities about yourself that are most likely to help you succeed in business.

_____

_____

_____

_____

_____

6. List eight words or phrases that you think others might use to describe you.

_____

_____

_____

_____

_____

_____

_____

_____

**C** Think now about the general image of American business managers. Assume the viewpoint of each person listed below, and suggest a single word or phrase that best describes business executives from that perspective.

| | |
|---|---|
| a ten-year old suburban boy or girl | _____ |
| a community college freshman | _____ |
| an individual stock investor | _____ |
| a Wall Street broker | _____ |
| the mayor of a midwestern town | _____ |
| a Western European college student | _____ |
| an environmentalist | _____ |
| a priest, rabbi, or minister | _____ |
| a novelist | _____ |
| a high ranking military officer | _____ |

**D** As a class, discuss the credibility of business speakers by addressing the following issues:

1. What conflicts, if any, exist between corporate profits and community welfare?
2. What conflicts, if any, exist between a corporate officer's accountability to shareholders, to employees, and to consumers?
3. What conflicts, if any, exist between the management philosophies of locally owned and nationally owned businesses?
4. What are the differences in perception of American business executives and those of other countries (e.g., Japan, France, Argentina, the Soviet Union, or South Africa)?

**E** As a class, return to the discussion of *persona*, and expand the list of credit-yielding qualities in a successful business speaker.

## SAMPLE SPEECH

This short speech was given by Libby James, president of TechData. This small graphics company employs eighteen workers and specializes in graphic design for technical publications. Over the eight years of its existence, the company has resisted diversification, choosing, instead, to focus its whole corporate effort on excellence in a given field. This speech was given by Mrs. James at the company's New Year's Eve party and seems off-the-cuff. The audience was standing in groups of two, three, or four, haphazardly arranged throughout a large living room. Numbering near forty, the workers and their guests were well dressed and amply supplied with refreshments. About one hour into the party, Mrs. James stepped onto the hearth and called for attention.

---

Since it is a rare occasion when we are all together like this, I think now would be a good time to go over a few end-of-the-year news items at TechData. I've got three pieces of good news and one piece of bad news.

The good news is that TechData just yesterday received the Commercial Designers Blumenberg Award for our layout of the TMB technical manual. That alone deserves a drink, HOWEVER, there's more.

The second piece of good news is that TechData increased our number of accounts by 30 percent over last year and took on four new employees. Now that, too, would call for a drink, but wait.

The third piece of good news is that we are now talking with an architect about designing a new simulation studio on the west lawn. And if there weren't some bad news to come, I'd say "cheers" right now.

The bad news is that with all this good news, I'm obliged to share the spoils. On Monday, you'll all find 10 percent bonus checks at your desk dated today.

Now—THAT calls for a drink.

---

This is an interesting little speech, perhaps considered odd in an anthology of business rhetoric. Nevertheless, when a company president addresses all employees, whether with champagne glass in hand or not, the occasion demands notice. In fact, this address meets several conditions of the typical business speech—it is delivered by a person in business to a business audience regarding a business subject.

There is a dual structure operating in this piece, sufficiently complicated to belie its apparently impromptu delivery. The speech is, at one time, both an elaborate toast and an extended good news-bad news joke. Both generic allusions are appropriate to the festive occasion, and the speaker sticks strictly to the expected formula of each.

Notice how Mrs. James encourages audience response throughout the speech. She assumes the double roles of host and president in the first sentence, both personae deserving attention. Then she sets up audience anticipation with an efficient promise of three pieces of good news and one bit of bad news. Each of the first three announcements is good news, indeed, probably eliciting a cheer or applause and deserving a drink—BUT. The constant counterpoint of the speaker's withheld drink to the list of reasons for celebration reminds listeners of bad news to come. Of course, the tongue-in-cheek irony and humor of delivery tell the audience that nothing truly terrible is coming. The apparently underplayed and begrudging announcement of bonus checks (i.e., "I'm obliged to share. . .") becomes the speech's climax. This announcement is guaranteed to elicit the most favorable response of all. The speaker provides closure to the address by completing the toast and inviting all to drink.

## DISCUSSION QUESTIONS

1. Speculate on Mrs. James's decision to save these business announcements for a social occasion rather than making them at the office or writing them in a memorandum. What are the communication benefits (or demerits) of her choice?

2. What is the probable effect upon audience response of these facts:
    a. listeners are standing together in small clusters?
    b. each listener has a glass in hand?
    c. the speaker is slightly elevated by standing on the hearth?
    d. spouses and other guests are present?
3. Was this speech made up on the spot or written and rehearsed in advance? What evidence does the transcript supply to support your conclusion?
4. Describe what you take to be the speaker's attitude toward her subject and toward her audience. Link each observation to features in the speech text.
5. The novelist John Cheever once said, "I can see a sip of sherry in a line of prose." Can you hear a sip of champagne in this speech? How much, if anything, has the speaker had to drink before delivering this address? Let several students try performances of the transcript. How high a level of intoxication will the language bear?

## HYPOTHETICAL SPEECH

Imagine yourself as the dean of a business college or the chairperson of a department of business administration. Your university is assessing the aims and usefulness of a general education curriculum—courses required of all undergraduates regardless of major. You have been asked to speak to the issue of general education requirements for undergraduate business majors before the president's advisory council. In a five-minute speech, build a case either for eliminating or for establishing such requirements. If you favor the general curriculum, argue for particular subjects that you consider necessary in the background of a broadly educated businessperson. If you advocate no general education requirements, defend this position with a rationale for the proper training of undergraduates who are business majors. Whichever position you defend, remember that your own credibility as an administrator and that of your educational program depend upon the validity and persuasiveness of your speech.

## SUMMARY

No business speech could succeed without a clear sense of direction provided by the speaker's intention. Of course, well-conceived intentions alone cannot ensure success unless conveyed properly to an audience. Later discussion will be devoted to the process of merger between speaker and listener. Our present interest is focused exclusively upon speech objectives from the speaker's point of view.

Naming the intentions of a given speech is, for the speaker, similar to setting production goals for a manufacturer. Both kinds of aims must be high enough to merit attaining, reasonable enough to fall within the reach of given circumstances, and specific enough to be measured. To determine the intention of a particular speech, the speaker should begin by answering three questions: What is the subject? What are its necessary limitations? What is my perspective toward this subject? Specific and concrete answers to these questions will provide a solid starting point for effective speech.

After naming a general intention, a speaker must concern himself or herself with the issue of credibility at every subsequent point, from research and composition through delivery. Credibility refers to the degree of trust that an audience invests in a given speaker and subject. Unless an individual merits and wins this believability, there is no chance of profitable communication. An initial, important step to ensure high ratings of reliability and trustworthiness is for the speaker to view himself or herself accurately—with insight, courage, and modesty. Self-awareness must be based upon a dependable knowledge of one's own skills and expertise, education and experience, vested interests and characteristic viewpoint. Self-recognition and acceptance, if specific and accurate, should help a speaker to acknowledge and accept the legitimate viewpoints of others, even when their beliefs conflict with the speaker's own. This ability to take on the perspective of others is critical to effective speech. A careful, clever speaker anticipates an audience's questions of credibility for every aspect of speech composition and delivery.

A believable speech offers facts before interpretation, is well organized, speaks with a human and personal vocabulary, and makes an integrated appeal to the whole listener. A believable speaker projects openness, has a fluent delivery, and is considerate of the audience. The achievements of speaker and speech credibility are not matters of deception or concealment but of expression and representation. A business speaker's initial tasks, then, are to articulate a specific intention and to discover all means available for winning the audience's confidence when fulfilling that speech objective.

# 4

# The Speaker: Aspects of Performance

Our study thus far has centered upon the speaker, his or her identity and context, intention, and credibility. We have been more interested in who is speaking than who is being addressed or what is being said. Before turning attention from the speaker to the audience and, later, to the text, we must introduce the difficult issue of performance. Delivery is the cause for anxiety in many speakers and, when done poorly, is the cause of even greater anxiety in audiences. In this chapter, we shall face squarely aspects of a business speaker's performance—the speech as a theatrical event, voice and movement, aesthetic considerations, and the performer's discipline of self-control.

## THE BUSINESS SPEECH AS A THEATRICAL EVENT

Some individuals in business, confronted by a public speaking assignment, delude themselves by thinking, "This is not a performance event." With such an assumption, the wary speaker seeks false comfort, and the lax speaker justifies inadequate preparation. In many ways, however, any public speaking situation *is* a theatrical event. It is so in the listeners' perceptions and ought to be viewed as such by the speaker as well. A speech, whether delivered casually to a few listeners or formally to many, offers counterparts to the theater's actor, audience, text, and setting. Communication effectiveness and impact are determined partly by the interplay among these dramatic elements.

A speaker is viewed by the audience as a kind of actor. This does not mean that a business speaker appears in costume, with makeup, delivering lines, and projecting character. Yet, each of these theatrical images suggests an aspect of audience perception analogous to public communication. An individual who stands up to speak commands attention, as does an actor. He or she projects a personality and viewpoint by each minute detail of presence. The speaker's physical appearance, typical gestures, use of space, vocal characteristics, and quality of engagement with an audience all *speak*. The well-trained actor communicates by more than mere words; he or she speaks by pause, inflection, and glance, by the color and cut of costume, and by the deft or clumsy handling of props. So, too, an effective business speaker acts. He or she knows the voracity of audience attention, the fact that an audience member will assign meaning to the smallest detail of performance—vocabulary, accent, rhythm, posture, grooming, and fashion. Only after a speaker comes to accept his or her role as a performer and to take advantage of every communicative possibility can that individual hope to create a consistent, compelling, and memorable presentation of self and subject.

Not only are business speeches made theatrical by the performer's role but by the audience's, as well. As when one goes to the theater with anticipation, the speech respondent arrives at a business occasion with a set of expectations. He or she has seen the publicity, as it were, and read the reviews. An audience member comes to the speech event knowing in advance something of the speaker and the subject. Depending upon advance notices, one expects little or much, and these expectations have a tangible effect upon perception. Speech and theater audiences are alike, too, in their varying modes of participation. According to the performance and the text, one is invited to sit back and observe, to enter a situation with laughter or empathy, or to participate actively in an ongoing plot by asking questions or joining in discussion. Just as the well-staged theatrical event seeks to direct and to control an audience's attention, so too does the effective public speaker.

When in later chapters we give focus to language and text, we shall see by detailed analogy how a good speech bears a resemblance to the well-made play. Both attempt to move their audiences through a sequence of complications to a crisis of decision and on to a climax of response. Both demand a sure sense of beginning, middle, and end with a structure and rhythm calculated to catch an audience up in the drama of human communication.

Our view of business speech as quasi-theater goes so far as to consider the speaking environment as a stage setting, itself an important element of communication. We know how critical to dramatic production are such features as audience seating, stage and house lighting, appropriate backdrops, set pieces and props, and a carefully designed space relationship between performer and viewer. If audiences for public speaking ascribe and accumulate meaning in ways similar to theater audiences, we must assume that variables in space and environment contribute to the speaker's success or failure.

The point in pressing this analogy between theater and speech is not to intimidate the business professional by an actor's expertise. It is to suggest the reality and complexity of audience perception. An individual hoping to communicate effectively and with force must be concerned with much more than getting the words out. He or she must orchestrate every aspect of performance to make a vital contribution to a speech and its impression upon an audience.

## VOICE AND MOVEMENT

At the most basic levels of performance, a speaker must learn to control voice and movement. These two skills correspond to the primary modes of audience perception—sound and sight—and both can be used to good effect. What a speaker sounds like and looks like can underscore, contradict, or distort what is said. In fact, it is rarely a simple matter to divorce the content of a speech from its manner of delivery. Audience members attribute meaning to voice and movement as well as to language and thought.

The basic vocal characteristics of a speaker may be described by five features—rate, pitch, rhythm, loudness, and quality. While total control over these is impossible, a practiced speaker can use his or her voice as a reliable and flexible instrument.

*Rate* is a measurement of speed: how fast does an individual speak? How many words per minute? There is no optimum pace for public speaking, though a median is approximately 140 words per minute. Different subject matters require different rates of speech depending upon level of vocabulary, complexity of thought, and the background of an audience. However, two guidelines should be followed. Never speak at such a fast rate that individual words cannot be articulated clearly, nor at such a slow rate that the logical flow of discourse cannot be followed. An exceedingly quick pace reduces speech to a meaningless patter; a speech delivered too slowly becomes disjointed in the mind of a listener. The second suggested guideline is to vary the pace of delivery. Any rate of speech maintained without change degenerates into droning. A good speaker can vary the tempo of delivery and ensure audience attention while underscoring his or her own intention.

*Pitch* refers to the musical notation of a voice. Most speakers have available to them a comfortable range of six to eight notes but typically use only two or three. Part of the training of any business speaker should include listening to oneself on audio tape. Many people are unaware of their own sound and rely on a very narrow range of pitch. They have a modal note, often too high, from which they stray infrequently, if at all. Such a monotone delivery carries over into the audience's perception of the speech as a whole. A monotonous performance brings a speech's thought and language to a level of monotony.

The optimum pitch for any speaker is near the low end of his or her comfortable range. Lower pitched voices are, as a rule, easier to listen to than those that are higher pitched. Pitching the voice two or three notes from the bottom of one's range allows ample space for movement up the scale for variety and emphasis, and allows some room for movement down the scale, too. If a speaker relies on a too-high modal pitch, the effect will be one of strain. To pitch the voice at its absolute lowest note produces a gravelly tone, which is hard to listen to for long. A practiced speaker returns most often in delivery to his or her lower range of pitch but uses the entire comfortable range for expression and vocal variety. Remember that the speaking voice enjoys the same range as a singing voice and that this whole range can be played to enhance communication.

*Rhythm* is a speaker's typical pattern of vocal movement and pause. Pace refers to the speed of discourse; rhythm refers to the continuity or flow of discourse. Rhythm is determined by the length of phrases, sentences, and paragraphs and by the larger structural units of a text. A speech moves—gathers momentum, propels itself forward, and slows down—just as an essay, a story, a play, or a musical composition moves. Speech is a performance occuring in time, and the speaker's rhythmic alternation between voice and pause helps to punctuate audience perception. A speaker's pauses must mark the logical grouping of words and can underscore a given idea with special emphasis. The best way to learn the function and value of rhythm in effective speech is to listen to master storytellers. They command audience attention and control rhythm by changing pace and using pause.

*Loudness* is a self-evident vocal quality. Individual voices display a characteristic volume. Those too soft must learn to project, to fill a space with sound and to reach all listeners with ease. Those too loud must learn to adapt their voices to the size of a room and to the number in an audience, to pull back and not to overpower listeners. In Chapter 11, in a discussion of convention speaking, we shall return to the subject of loudness and the use of microphones.

*Quality* or timbre refers to the manner of vocal production, to the physical apparatuses that propel and shape human sound. An individual speaker cannot change the length of vocal cords, the size or construction of a mouth, or the many points of resonation within a body. However, any speaker can support his or her voice with good breath control, precise articulation, and a personal awareness of one's own vocal resonance.

This survey of voice characteristics suggests a number of performance options available to the good speaker. No one can persuade or move an audience solely by a rich and pleasing voice. However, a dull or offensive voice can, and often does, undermine the impact of an otherwise effective speech. A speaker's rate, pitch, rhythm, loudness, and vocal quality offer a wide range for expression. Emphasis, pause, and inflection are a speaker's punctuation and italics, without which composition and delivery would be unintelligible. The voice itself can determine meaning. Audiences listen to manners of speech to pick up cues to a speaker's attitude. Slight variations in tone can indicate sarcasm or sincerity, a teasing or serious viewpoint, conviction or apathy. Perhaps most important to the business speaker, vocal control can assure an audience of one's confidence and authority.

Just as the voice communicates apart from, and in conjunction with language, so too does the body. Every movement of a speaker is an aspect of performance and contributes to meaning for an audience. Facial expression, gesture, the use of space, and proximity to an audience all speak, regardless of the speaker's intention or degree of control over these behaviors. So important is the body's nonverbal communication that audiences usually rely on it to temper and to test the validity of a speaker's words. That is, when a speaker says one thing but the body says another, by nervous mannerisms, a twitch, or even undue perspiration, an audience tends to believe the visual rather than the aural communication.

When our attention turns in the next three chapters to aspects of audience perception, we shall return to the significant differences between what an audience sees and what they hear. It is important now, however, to acknowledge a speaker's obligation to present a total and consistent impression. A public speaker *is* a performer, whether or not one enjoys or appreciates the role. To be an effective speaker, one must become a good performer. Again, this mandate does not invite deceit or duplicity but insists upon an accurate representation of the speaker's viewpoint and the subject's scope. Good performance does not conceal; it reveals.

## THE AESTHETICS OF BUSINESS COMMUNICATION

In the last chapter, we defined "persona" and discussed several qualities essential to the makeup of a model business speaker. The present interest in delivery demands corresponding standards for performance. These are aesthetic expectations, ideals in the business speaker's art. Here are five principles of good performance.

First, an effective speech is *dynamic* both in its content and its delivery. In the same way that a healthy commercial enterprise must move forward, a successful speech should be in constant motion and have a sure sense of direction. In fact, audiences may judge the liveliness of a business by the communication dynamism of its executives. Dynamic delivery demands a firm grasp on a lean outline, concentrated attention on the subject at hand, and alertness to audience response.

Second, business speech must be *practical* in every aspect of its composition and performance. Again, this communication standard corresponds to commercial expectations. The same qualities deemed virtuous (and profitable) in business pay dividends in speech delivery. A good speech must be to the point, its delivery marked by no nonsense. The ornamentation and elegance of artistic performance usually do not serve well the pragmatic ends of business communication.

Third, an effective speech is *efficient* in its use of language and gesture. Just as a good text does not waste words, an efficient performance invests motion and space frugally. Economy of gesture and movement means that a speaker should use the simplest and most direct approach to communication at every point in a speech.

The fourth measurement of business performance may be termed *sophistication*. This standard includes high intelligence, a broad outlook, and contemporary awareness. These qualities show themselves in a speech text by vocabulary, evidence, points of reference, and allusions to the nonbusiness world. In performance, sophistication becomes apparent in a speaker's bearing, manners, clothing, and address to the audience.

A fifth aesthetic expectation of the business speaker is *control*. He or she must at all times be in command of self and subject. The degree of control is evident in mannerisms, fluency of speech, handling of notes and visual aids, and eye contact with the audience. A good speaker must be so sure of himself or herself and the subject at hand that he or she can concentrate fully on engagement with the audience, the ongoing communication.

## A PERFORMER'S DISCIPLINES

To master the expectations of good business speech, an individual may practice several disciplines, habits of preparation and performance. The first is to maintain constant vigilance over one's own use of the language. Careful thinking and precise speaking are capacities closely linked to one another. One cannot turn language on and off, expecting to use it well in public if it is not well practiced in private. A good business speaker builds credibility on a reputation for careful communication. Objective discourse and self-expression can be enhanced by disciplines of wide reading (not only business publications), conscientious conversation, and competent writing.

A second discipline necessary to the business speaker is planning and scheduling. Any speech assignment may be broken down into a series of tasks: objective, research, analysis, composition, practice, and delivery. Adequate time must be allotted to each phase of preparation, and this distribution requires careful planning with personal deadlines. Nothing undermines speech effectiveness so much as inadequate preparation or a speaker's feeling of not being ready.

A third set of disciplines may seem mundane but is, in fact, quite important—a sensible routine before the speech event. Some speakers, to overcome anxious jitters, upset their normal life routine by smoking more than usual, sleeping less, or changing a typical pattern of food and beverage consumption. These disruptions to normalcy have the opposite effect of calming a speaker: they increase a state of agitation. Self-control is developed partly by a sensible life routine maintained through periods of ease and crisis.

A fourth discipline, perhaps most important, may be described by a pair of attitudes. A successful speaker can overcome debilitating stage fright by caring enough about his or her subject and audience. If one has something to say of great importance and cares deeply that others should understand the subject too, stage fright is minimized and may actually lend a keen edge to delivery. The stagewise speaker learns to concentrate on what is being said now, not on what is coming or what was said earlier. He or she thinks primarily about the subject matter, secondly about audience perception, and lastly about himself or herself. To reverse the order, to wonder constantly what one sounds like or looks like and to think about how one feels at the moment of speaking, subverts communication and increases anxiety.

Throughout this chapter, we have placed the speaker's own person in a rather hot spotlight. Competent performance is not difficult when one accepts the performer's role and its obligations. Fulfilling these responsibilities is often a matter of careful and objective observation and applying common sense to choices of communication. Speech strategies must take into account the multiple modes of audience perception. And the good speaker takes responsibility for orchestrating those perceptions.

## EXERCISES

**A**   This first exercise is a questionnaire asking you to speculate upon, and fill out the dimensions of, a theatrical metaphor for business speech. An acquaintance once claimed that she could tell a college professor from a business executive because the latter shined his or her shoes—such is the detail of performance perception. Imagine yourself now as the casting director of a movie that calls for two believable business executives, one man and one woman. In casting these roles, consider who, among popular film and TV actors, could best portray the qualities of a successful executive.

1. On the basis of *voice* alone, what performer would you cast in the female role?




the male role?




2. On the basis of *appearance* alone (i.e., stature, bearing, grooming, and fashion), what performer would you cast in the female role?

Who would you cast in the male role?

3. On the basis of *movement* alone (i.e., gesture and walk), what performer would you cast in the female role?

Who would you cast in the male role?

4. Now imagine that you were casting a comic film and needed to find two actors whose performances would be *least* representative of the successful business executive. Who would you cast in the female role?

Who would you cast in the male role?

5. As a class, share your answers and analyze the specific performance qualities that you consider appropriate and inappropriate, credible and incredible in a business executive. Specify manners of speech, fashion, bearing, gesture, movement, and other performance details. Are there differences between your expectations of men and women? If so, what are they, and why do they exist?

**B**   Here is a short excerpt from a speech delivered by M.T. Hopkins, the new president of Rollster Enterprises, at an early retirement dinner for the outgoing president. Read the paragraph silently, then follow the performance directions below.

> Words cannot adequately express my own feelings on this occasion nor would it be easy to record in language your contribution to this company's reputation. Under your leadership, Rollster has diversified its interests, entered international markets, and doubled its number of employees. You have set us on a straight course that will dictate development well into the future.

These three sentences represent only a small part of the whole speech, purposely taken out of context. Rehearse aloud several different interpretations of this brief passage and note carefully differences of perception in response to specific vocal characteristics.

1. Let one student try the passage at a very slow rate of speech in a deeply pitched voice.
2. Let another another student try the speech at a much faster tempo.
3. Let a third student perform with exaggerated pauses before the words "contribution," "reputation," "leadership," and "dictate."
4. Try alternate performances of the same words, which would indicate the following speaker attitudes:
    a. deep appreciation and respect.
    b. slight embarrassment and discomfort at the forced retirement of a predecessor.
    c. heavy sarcasm, as though delivered at a mock ceremony with the "guest of honor" not present.
5. What difference to perception would it make if the speech were delivered in a dialect from Mississippi? Michigan? Texas? Massachusetts? New York? South Carolina? or any other regional speech pattern?

**C** Review the current TV advertisments selling products, services, and other business interests. List the three commercials that you consider to represent best their business objectives:

1.
2.
3.

List three commercials that you consider failures in their attempt to represent well a given product, service, or other interest.

1.
2.
3.

Now go back to our discussion of the aesthetics of business communication and recall the qualities of dynamism, practicality, efficiency, sophistication, and control. Using these terms and ideas, analyze what makes your commercial choices succeed or fail.

**D** Think about the general life disciplines that are likely to produce effective business speakers. List ten works of literature that any well-educated person should have read. Do not offer a rote list of classics. Be prepared to defend your list with a specific rationale for the value of each title.

1.
2.
3.
4.
5.
6.
7.
8.
9.
10.

To keep abreast of current political, scientific, and cultural developments, list five journals or magazines that a business speaker should read regularly.

  1.
  2.
  3.
  4.
  5.

To keep abreast of current national and international business developments, list five periodicals that a businessperson should read regularly.

  1.
  2.
  3.
  4.
  5.

In one, well-developed paragraph, state and defend your rationale for a business executive's proper attitude toward routine physical exercise. Be specific in your recommendations and provide serious reasons in their support.

## SAMPLE SPEECH

Here is the transcript of a brief speech delivered without manuscript or notes. The speaker is the president of a large insurance company, and the occasion is the opening of a week's leadership training conference for prospective managers. The audience numbers forty, all individuals selected by merit for the week-long seminar. The prospective managers have been flown to corporate headquarters in Atlanta for the conference.

---

Once there was a young country preacher who, arriving at his small church on Sunday morning, was surprised to find only one person there—an old farmer. Not sure what to do in this situation, the young minister asked the farmer, "What do you think, Brother Sesser, should I go ahead with my sermon with only one person here?"

The farmer sat silent for awhile and then answered, "Well, if I went to the pasture of a morning to feed hay and only one cow showed up, I'd feed her."

The young minister, with his confidence built up by this remark, went ahead with the service and preached his sermon from beginning to end, just as planned. Afterwards, he spoke to the farmer again: "What did you think of my sermon, Brother Sesser?"

The farmer answered, "Well, if I went to the pasture of a morning to feed hay and only one cow showed up, I wouldn't feed her the whole damned load."

Ladies and gentlemen, I'm happy to see this sizeable group of forty because over the next five days, we intend to feed you the "whole damned load."

Each of you has been chosen by a regional manager to attend this week of special training. The company has paid your air fare and provided accommodations that we trust are to your liking. And we have brought in six of the best instructors available from two international corporations and four universities to teach our seminars on management and leadership. Our investment in each of you and your future careers has been substantial, with the promise of even greater returns to come—high dividends for you, for your family, and for our corporate enterprise. But this idea of investment in persons is hardly new to any of you, I know. You could not have got to this point in your careers without hard work, personal discipline, and considerable sacrifice. The fact of your presence here this week indicates our recognition of your achievements and our appreciation of your loyalty to this company and its objectives.

In the days to come, you'll work a rigorous schedule of class time, discussions, interviews, reading, and writing. While you may find the load heavy, this is no basic training. This, ladies and gentlemen, is our officers candidate school, and the successful graduates can look forward to a future of increased responsibility and greater rewards.

By the time you leave Atlanta, you'll feel like you've been fed the "whole damned load," but I've got just enough farm-smarts in *me* to say a short piece and shut up quick. I'll get a chance to meet each of you individually during the week for a half-hour interview, and I'll see all of you together in various of the group meetings. For now, welcome to Atlanta. Welcome to the home office. And glad to have you here.

This short address offers a particularly interesting example of speech performance. Because we do not know the speaker's identity or personality apart from this transcript, judgments must be made on the sole bases of *what* he or she says and *how* he or she speaks. The language and voice of this particular address could not have come from just any speaker: they are distinctive and they direct attention, for good or ill, to a distinctive speaker.

The first third of the speech is devoted to one anecdotal joke, and two later references are made to it. This was a risky decision for a communicator to make because the effectiveness of his or her speech depends so heavily upon audience perception of that joke: Is it funny? Is it appropriate to the audience and to the occasion? Is it representative of the company's highest officer? And the anecdote in print is at least good enough to suggest that its impact in speech will depend entirely upon its delivery.

Presumably, the objectives of this address are (1) to introduce the company president, (2) to praise those individuals selected for management training, (3) to encourage an enthusiastic attitude toward the week's learning experience, and (4) to make the audience feel at home and welcome in corporate headquarters.

## DISCUSSION QUESTIONS

1. Draw a profile of the speaker implicit in this speech by answering the following questions. Support each supposition with a specific reference to the text.
   a. Is the speaker male or female?
   b. How old is the speaker?
   c. What is the speaker's attitude toward the audience and the occasion?
2. Speculate upon the speaker's voice in performance. Does he or she have a distinctive accent? Is the speech delivered at a slow or quick pace? What differences do quality of voice and manner have on the likely impact of the joke?
3. Is the joke appropriate to the purposes of this speech? Discuss its communicative advantages and disadvantages.
4. Discuss the appropriateness and value of the military metaphors in the speech (i.e., "basic training" and "officers candidate school").
5. If you were a young career person in this speech audience, what impressions would the speaker leave with you?

## HYPOTHETICAL SPEECH

In several recent instances of international diplomacy, issues of national policy have conflicted with specific business interests. For example, say that the government imposes trade sanctions on a given nation. This forces a corporation either to violate a contract to deliver to that nation or to violate a government sanction and honor the business contract. Put yourself in the position of a corporation officer for an international company with headquarters in the United States. In a four-to five-minute speech, explain your general position regarding business loyalties to governments and to clients. Do not skirt the issue with platitudes and generalities. Go to its center, and support your position with specific examples.

## SUMMARY

Whether or not a businessperson likes public communication or is comfortable in the role of speaker, there is no getting away from the performance obligations of a speech assignment. The business speech delivered before a large or small audience is a theatrical event. Successful speakers recognize this fact and use its implications to good effect in their composition and delivery. Any speech is made theatrical not so much by the speaker's intention as by an audience's perception. To the minds of listeners, every speech offers equivalents to the theater's actor, audience, text, and setting.

Everything about a speaker—appearance, voice, gesture, and movement—says something to an audience. Effective speech depends as much upon nonverbal behavior and paralanguage (e.g., tone of voice, inflection, pause, and other vocal characteristics) as it does upon carefully chosen words. To make these various cues to overall meaning consistent with a speaker's intentions, rather than contradictory, one must become a self-aware performer. Just as the speaker plays an actor's role, the listener assumes an audience perspective. At the least, this means that prior expectations and knowledge of a speech event will have an effect upon its communication. Likewise, the dramatic structure of a text and all environmental aspects of a speech setting will contribute to audience perception.

A speaker's performance responsibilities are met foremost by careful control over voice and movement. Vocal characteristics of rate, pitch, rhythm, loudness, and quality can be used to underscore meaning and to punctuate discourse. A listener ascribes intention and significance to tone of voice as much as to language. Similarly, every body movement in performance speaks—facial expression, gesture, the use of space, and proximity to an audience.

Whatever the unique circumstances of a given performance assignment, all business speech should be marked by common aesthetic principles that correlate communication behavior with good business practice. An effective speech and a compelling speaker should be characterized by dynamism, practicality, efficiency, sophistication, and control. To achieve these qualities, a speaker must practice constant disciplines of good communication: vigilance over one's use of language, careful planning and scheduling, a sensible routine of relaxation before a speech event, and genuine care for one's subject and audience.

In this chapter and the preceding two, we have looked at the business speech from a speaker's viewpoint—his or her identity and context, intention and credibility, and performance. However, this singular viewpoint alone is insufficient to describe speech communication. As suggested at the outset of our study, real communication depends upon interaction among speaker, audience, and text. Because a speaker is the most visible partner in this relationship, it seemed sensible to start with his or her presence. Attention turns now to issues of audience perception.

# 5

# The Audience: Analysis and Projection

       Speech communication would be a much simpler (and duller) process if its success depended solely upon a speaker and his or her intentions. However, no matter how careful a speaker's planning and precise one's thinking, real communication demands the creative contribution of an audience. There is no "A" for effort given to a speaker who satisfies his or her own standards for clear expression while utterly baffling an audience. Speech merit can only be measured as the territory of shared meaning between a speaker and a listener. Real communication results from a partnership in which both speaker and audience make an investment and from which each participant may share the profits (or suffer the losses). In this and the succeeding two chapters, our attention turns to the role of audience perception in speech communication.

       The specific interest of this chapter is the identity of audiences for business speech. Just as we tried to clarify the speaker's role in earlier discussion, we shall begin a consideration of audience with the basic question of identity. We shall move on, then, to the related matters of projection and temporal perception.

## IDENTITY AND ANALYSIS

The possible profiles of prospective audiences for business speech are as broad and various as the strata of society. Almost no individual worldwide could be excluded from the pool of potential consumers. The mention of business speech brings to mind a number of typical audiences: committees, boards, departments, sales representatives, shareholders, clients, potential customers, and union members, to name a few. But there are many other potential audiences. Consumers in general are interested in statements of corporate profit, assurances of material and design safety, and promises of product reliability. Regulatory agencies monitor the public communication of businesses in order to judge truth in advertising and to assess any conflicts of interest between corporate and community welfare. Local residents neighboring a business enterprise become keenly attentive to announcements of expansion or other changes in operation. Competitors scan all public pronouncements. Financial institutions and private investors watch and listen to business speech. School boards, civic and service organizations, churches, and charities have an interest in business speech. Perhaps the least acknowledged audience for public communication are children; they have easy access to speech through news broadcasts, advertisements, and the distillation of adult conversation. Just as no topic can be ruled out as inappropriate to business, neither can a segment of the population be ignored as a primary or secondary audience for business speech.

With this enormous range of backgrounds, interests, and knowledge among potential audiences, a speaker's communication task may seem nearly impossible to fulfill. Obviously, the same language, structure, and tone of voice are not appropriate to all audiences. What may be perfectly clear and useful to one listener may be confusing, worthless, or even offensive to another. Because the identity and perception of an audience play their parts in communication, a speaker must make all choices of composition and delivery with a fair view of the intended listener. As a major planning phase of any speech assignment, thus, one must speculate upon audience profiles and analyze their implications.

In some cases, an audience is familiar to the speaker even to the point of knowing their names, titles, salaries, and idiosyncracies. On other occasions, the speaker faces an auditorium of foreign faces concealing as much as they reveal of their identities behind a placid smile or an expressionless visage. In any case, whether speaking before friends or enemies, superiors or subordinates, men or women, old or young, an effective speaker must answer basic questions of audience identity and should adapt communication strategies accordingly.

Audience identification begins with a basic demographic profile. On the basis of whatever information is available, a speaker must try to answer these questions:

How many audience members will be present?
Of what age range?
Of what sex?

Of what race, ethnic background, or religious persuasion?
From what region or locality?
With what level of education?

Without imposing unfair stereotypes, it may be assumed that audiences of different ages, sex, region, or education not only may have different interests but also may respond to different appeals; they will bring to a speech different personal "dictionaries" of experience and meaning. Demographic data serve to sketch the broad contours of an audience profile, and a sensitive, clever speaker can fill in several specific features by asking the right questions and acquiring sufficient information.

A second category of inquiry about speech audiences includes all questions related to business context. For example,

Is the audience comprised primarily of colleagues, subordinates, or superiors in the corporate hierarchy?
What organizational roles do audience members play (e.g., manager, competitor, shareholder, salaried or hourly worker)?
What is an audience's attitudinal range of commitment, loyalty, or opposition to the business enterprise represented?

A third class of questions that a speaker must answer in order to project accurately an audience's identity centers upon the listeners' relationship to a speech topic. Audiences come to a speech event with a perceptual structure shaped by who they are outside the business context and who they are inside the organization (our first two categories of inquiry), and they come with a set of predispositions toward a given topic. To assess these accurately, a speaker should ask the following questions:

What prior knowledge of the topic does the audience possess?
Is the audience familiar with a technical vocabulary or special meanings for words associated with the topic?
What viewpoint and range of attitudes toward the topic are represented in the audience?
What is the depth of commitment among audience members to predispositions regarding the topic?
What personal experience have audience members had with the topic?

Another important area for consideration when drawing an audience profile is the typical attitude of a listener to the speaker and the corporation represented.

How much prior contact has the audience had with this speaker?
What are the most likely assumptions an audience might make about the speaker's viewpoint from his or her title, introduction, and other prior knowledge?
What images, attitudes, and perspectives does the audience associate with the corporation represented?

Finally, a speaker must assess the overall viewpoint of an audience in terms of their vested interests:

What do listeners have to gain or lose by adopting the speaker's perspective and responding to his or her appeal?

What changes of predisposition would be required for an audience to respond affirmatively to the speaker's viewpoint? How threatening or otherwise difficult would these changes be to make?

In what ways are a speaker's topic and viewpoint in cooperation or conflict with a listener's other interests?

Answers to these five categories of questions outline an audience profile. Where little information is available to the speaker, one must make some reliable guesses regarding audience identity. No speaker can hope to share a broad common ground with an audience without knowing who they are and where they are coming from. Questions of identity must cover demographic information, business context, prior knowledge of a topic, perceptions of speaker and corporate credibility, and the vested interests of audience members.

## SPEAKER PROJECTION AND THE IMPLIED AUDIENCE

A speaker's accurate probes into audience identity can serve as reliable guides to many choices of speech composition and delivery. If a speaker can anticipate listener attitudes, knowledge, needs, and interests, these will become the common ground for real engagement. Part of a speaker's task is to project his or her awareness of an audience into the language, structure, and manner of a speech.

One useful image for understanding the concept of projection is that of an *implied audience*. In much the same way that a speaker's appearance and behavior project a personality and imply a perspective, the language and style of a speech imply a certain understanding of the audience. A speaker's assumptions about his or her listeners—their knowledge and interests, intelligence and needs—become manifest at various points in a speech. An audience is implied by the conscious or unconscious expectations that a speaker builds into the speech. If these expectations are based upon an accurate assessment of the audience and are projected clearly, listeners will feel as though they are addressed directly and will be likely to give willing attention. If, however, the implied audience for a speech is not a good match of the real audience (i.e., if expectations are based upon false assumptions), listeners will resist the speaker's communication. The notion of an implied audience affects public communication in the same way that projected attitudes affect interpersonal communication. One does not respond well to any speaker who has made false assumptions about who the listener is.

An individual's projection of the implied audience is made manifest at every point in a speech and is particularly obvious on four dimensions—information, diction, manner of delivery, and rhetorical structure. Audience projection is nowhere more evident than in a speaker's choice of *information*. Deciding which data to include and which to exclude, how great an explanation of an idea is necessary, and how much introduction to a concept is required all demand the accurate assessment of an audience's knowledge. The importance of a speaker's choices of information may be made clear if you recall the last public occasion you attended when a speaker failed to project an accurate profile of the listeners. If an audience's prior knowledge is underestimated, a speaker may bore listeners with unnecessary information or may patronize them with simple explanations. On the other hand, if a speaker overestimates prior knowledge, he or she can scare an audience off or intimidate them with a barrage of new facts, unfamiliar data, or technical explanations. Real communication demands of the speaker some sensible calculation of an audience's prior knowledge and corresponding good sense in selecting appropriate information. The information required to reach one audience may be totally unsuited to another, thus the crucial importance of audience identification and accurate projection. The profile of an implied audience must match, at all critical points, the identities of real listeners.

A second speech dimension that reflects certain assumptions about an audience is the speaker's *diction* or word choices. Proper language usage, like the effective choice of information, must take into account prior knowledge. In addition, word selection indicates a speaker's real sensitivity to his or her listeners and to a specific public occasion. In most business situations, vocabulary should be chosen for its straightforward, unambiguous impact. In literature or dramatic performance, words often serve best that can mean two or three things simultaneously to an audience. Such double meanings are rarely useful in business communication; unequivocal language is the medium of most commercial exchange. While business speech ought never to be haughty, cold, or impersonal, language ought to reflect its user's common sense, intelligence, and deliberate reserve. As observed in our earlier discussion of credibility, effective speech behavior corresponds to efficient business practice—at every point it must be both practical and farsighted. In vocabulary choices, a speaker must avoid the extremes of overformality or unwarranted intimacy—both inappropriate to public speech communication—and one must eschew any word choice likely to offend an audience by its racism, sexism, or elitism.

A speaker's *manner of delivery*, from tone of voice to physical bearing, can also project his or her assumptions about an audience's identity. The performance characteristics discussed in Chapter 4 particularly indicate a speaker's personal regard or level of respect for an audience. If a listener feels directly addressed with real eye contact and a perceived sincerity of voice, one attends willingly to what is said. When a speaker never looks up from his or her manuscript and reads with an impersonal, insincere, or monotonous voice, a listener makes a like investment in the communication. Worse, a cavalier disregard for the listener reflected in a speaker's flippant performance behavior is likely to irritate and produce negative results. In short, manner of delivery can project a speaker's commitment to both subject and listener and can, thereby, encourage similar commitment in the audience's response. Performance itself projects a speaker's expectations of the audience.

## THE AUDIENCE'S TEMPORAL PERCEPTION

A fourth dimension of audience projection deserves its own heading, namely, rhetorical structure. Two later chapters will be devoted entirely to various arrangements of speech texts and their persuasive appeals. The purpose in introducing the subject here is to show how audience analysis and projection must help to determine all organizational choices in a speech.

What is most important to understand about the art of oratory is its temporal nature. Speech is time-bound and its perception by listeners also occurs over time. One does not perceive speech primarily in spatial terms as one does, say, architecture or sculpture. One responds to speech primarily in time frames as one would respond to music, dance, drama, or a well-told story. This temporal aspect of speech perception makes a real difference to a speaker's approach to any assignment.

When listening to public speech, one is moved to change (or is hardened to resist change). A speaker's task is to envision some desired end point for audience perception (e.g., a new level of information, awareness of a new product, an altered attitude, or a commitment to purchase). This end cannot be achieved all at once; change requires a sequence of small perceptual steps taken over time. It is as important for a speaker to know where his or her audience is likely to be at the beginning of a speech as it is to determine where they should be at the end. Assigning a specific communication goal in terms of audience response represents the speaker's objective. Determining where persuasion must begin is a function of audience analysis. Only after an accurate assessment of listener identity and a reasonable projection of some intended response have been determined can a speaker design the intermediate steps in a rhetorical sequence.

Every piece of information about an audience and each calculated guess of a listener's predispositions can contribute to speech effectiveness. A speaker projects his or her knowledge of and attitude toward an audience by every word choice, by the selection of information, by manner of delivery, and by a speech's pattern of organization. If the implied audience created by these assumptions and choices matches the actual audience's profile, real communication is facilitated. If audience analysis is neglected or mistaken, a speaker's misprojection of an implied audience can undermine communication and have a negative impact on individual and corporate credibility.

## EXERCISES

**A**   Most of the practice speeches given in this course will be presented in your classroom before your classmates. They comprise your audience. As a beginning exercise in audience analysis, answer the following questions as best you can, making a reasonable guess when solid information is unavailable. Do not consult one another; let each student fill in the blanks with his or her own speculation.

1. What is the age range of this classroom speech audience?

_____

2. What is the average number of years of work experience among your classmates?

_____

3. What is the range of economic backgrounds represented in this audience?

_____

4. What is the range of regional backgrounds among your classmates?

_____

5. What three works of literature would you surmise that all (or most) of your classmates have read?

_____

_____

_____

6. What two films released within the past year would you guess that most members of the class have seen?

_____

_____

7. If you were to choose one speech topic guaranteed to interest the whole class, what would it be?

_____

8. If you were to choose one speech topic guaranteed to bore the class, what would it be?

_____

9. How many of your classmates attend church regularly?

_____

10. How many of your classmates own stock?

_____

These questions represent only a small fraction of the demographic data and background information you might need to know about an audience before delivering an effective speech. As a class, tabulate your responses, and note any critical discrepancies among answers or between perception and reality. Then discuss what specific differences these kinds of information might make to a speaker's preparation.

**B**   Read the following list of sex-biased words and suggest sex-neutral alternatives in the spaces provided.

| businessman | _____ |
| chairman | _____ |
| housewife | _____ |
| foreman | _____ |
| salesman | _____ |
| manpower | _____ |
| actress | _____ |
| layman | _____ |
| congressman | _____ |
| manmade | _____ |

**C**   As a demonstration of an audience's temporal perception, use the following two-part critique form for one classroom speech. Unlike most forms that call for audience responses to a speaker's effectiveness, this form asks you to observe your own behavior as an audience member. This is no easy exercise because it demands objective self-awareness. You must make conscious processes of listening and viewing that usually occur unconsciously—by habit or, apparently, by instinct.

The left column of Part One lists a typical sequence of speaker behaviors; the right column has blanks for your response. As carefully and accurately as possible, record what you are thinking and feeling as the speech progresses. For instance, the first impression made by a speaker is when he or she walks to the front of the group. That is when communication begins. You are already forming judgments before the speaker utters one word. What are you thinking and feeling? Your responses may include thoughts, feelings, questions, comments, arguments, or whatever else is really going on in your mind and perception.

Part Two may be filled out *after* the speech.

Be sure to read Part One *before* trying the exercise.

---

### Part One
#### (to be filled out during the speech)

| *Speaker's Behavior* | *Your Response* |
|---|---|
| 1. Walk to the front of room; first sight of general appearance, dress, and physical bearing. | 1. |
| 2. First sentence of speech. | 2. |
| 3. First major point. | 3. |
| 4. Evidence, example, or other supporting material. | 4. |
| 5. Second major point. | 5. |
| 6. Third major point. | 6. |
| 7. Conclusion. | 7. |
| 8. Walk back to seat. | 8. |

Part Two
(to be filled out after the speech)

1. Describe your attitude toward the topic at the beginning of this speech.

2. Describe your attitude toward the topic at the end of the speech.

3. Describe your attitude toward the speaker at the beginning of the speech (i.e., your perceptions of his or her knowledge, authority, and credibility).

4. Describe your attitude toward the speaker at the end of the speech.

5. What specific words, references, or arguments stick out in your memory of the speech?

## SAMPLE SPEECH

Here is the transcript of an address delivered by Alexander Rawleigh to an audience of three hundred representatives of various consumer groups. Its introduction should set the context for your reading.

---

"Matching the Stereotype"
An Address Before the Los Angeles Better Business Association


by
Alexander Rawleigh, Jr.
Chairman, DATACORE


When I was invited to speak before your group, I responded with a mixture of negative emotions:

—*defensiveness* because business executives and consumer advocates are popularly pitted in adversary roles;
—*anxiety* because I'm not equipped or willing to defend THE business point of view as though such a generalization were valid;
—*trepidation* because I'm not fond of public speaking and least so before a potentially hostile audience; and
—*suspicion* because I didn't like the odds.

All of these negative feelings arise from a stereotypical picture of consumerism and commercialism as mutually exclusive interests. This dichotomy is by now so prevalent in our cultural perceptions as to be accepted without question or pause by young people entering the marketplace and entering business enterprises. Overcoming these initial negative responses to your invitation was my urgent and deeply felt conviction that the supposed enmity between consumer interests and business interests is a preposterous lie grown to mythic magnitude and threatening to undermine the real interests of both business and consumer. I am, therefore, grateful, very grateful, for the opportunity to speak to you today.

Rather than skirting the issue of our alleged enmity, I intend to address it, to attack the smokescreen illogic of its premises. I've titled my address "Matching the Stereotype," and I want to discuss the debilitating images that limit both business managers and consumers alike.

Let's look first at the most extreme case of consumer paranoia of business executives. According to popular myth, the business executive may be characterized by six features:

1. He is, first and foremost, a man.
2. He is, by definition, rich and, by extension, uncaring, aloof, pompous, and elitist.
3. He is concerned more with profit than product safety, more with markets than persons, more with balance sheets than community welfare.
4. He operates on the fringes of national and international law with a lobbying power to twist loopholes in legislation whenever convenient.
5. He has little if any personal integrity—willing when circumstances present themselves to give and accept bribes, payoffs, and kickbacks.
6. He would, at a dinner party of nonbusiness professionals, show himself to be an utter bore, if not an ass.

While I grant that this profile represents an extreme stereotype, perhaps you'll grant that it's not so extreme a view as to be utterly comic. While I expected and accept your laughter at these descriptions, you encourage me to persist by the fact that you didn't applaud.

Now let's look together at this stereotyped profile and test its accuracy. I refuse to take on the job of defense attorney painting a beatific picture of American business, but I am willing to dispute with what vigor I can muster several of these popular assumptions.

First, it is accurate to picture the upper echelons of American business as occupied primarily by men rather than women. The fact that this is changing rapidly promises redress to an historical imbalance in the not too distant future. Furthermore, the notable success of women executives has brought to several corporations a new vision of productivity, creativity, and (to some extent) accountability.

The second feature of our profile, that business executives are personally rich is also, one hopes, accurate. I shall argue, however, that the connotations of wealth—a lack of human caring, pomposity, and elitism—are not inevitable consequences and represent an oversimplification of what is, in fact, a complicated and often agonizing personal and moral condition.

Any business executive who fits neatly into the third category of the stereotype, placing profits above persons, will not long remain a manager because the two interests cannot be separated. All business activity ultimately serves people, and only high quality products and services will last in the marketplace. While this platitude is true, I can't deny many instances in which business enterprises have not served the public well. My point is that such businesses are not good businesses measured against human *or* economic standards. One need only witness the bankruptcy of three major asbestos firms in recent weeks to validate the argument.

The fourth and fifth features of our profile have to do with personal and corporate integrity in relation to national and international law. Again, abuses abound and are well documented in courts of law and properly publicized by the media. But the stereotype is not, in fact, typical, and the no-win situations of Clausen Industries and others lately indicate the complexity and frequent conflicts inherent in corporate compliance with all applicable laws.

The final feature of this villainous portrait of the American business executive is that he is, most likely, an utter bore at most dinner parties. To this I would have to agree wholeheartedly.

If we were to turn the tables and draw a composite picture of the worst case of business paranoia toward consumer advocates, we could paint an equally unflattering portrait. Such individuals are thought to be naïve, ill-informed, narrow-minded, simplistic in their thinking, shallow in their emotions, timid in their courage, and short-sighted in their vision of the future. You know the images as well as I and surely they hurt as much when applied to you as the images of uncaring, selfishness, and profiteering hurt when applied to me.

What worries me terribly about these polarized portraits is not that either one is utterly false when applied to certain individuals. My concern is that both sets of assumptions are false when applied to business at large or to consumer groups across the board. What is most unfair is that these stereotypes become not *descriptions* of behavior and viewpoint but become *prescriptions* for behaviors and attitudes. To the extent that these images are allowed to become expectations an even greater rift grows between constituencies who ought to come closer and closer together.

I, for one, refuse to acknowledge any natural enmity between commercial interests and consumer interests. When such enmity exists in private business or among the public, it is debilitating to the separate interests of each group and devastating to the common interests of both. Let us not be induced into a war where no victory is possible and where great losses are inevitable. Instead, let us negotiate with vigor and candor our mutual concerns and hope, in the future, for a profitable cooperation.

---

This speech is interesting on several levels, not the least being its projection of an implied audience. Notice that the speaker has made several assumptions about his listeners and has allowed these to come to the surface of language and thought. Right from the start he acknowledges some discomfort in his role and then argues that his very misgivings exemplify the theme of his speech—that stereotypes inhibit negotiation and cooperation between business and consumer. Discuss the following questions and issues in an effort to assess the speech's strengths and weaknesses.

## DISCUSSION QUESTIONS

1. What do you take to be the speech's primary purpose?
2. Describe the implied audience within this speech. Be specific and support your answers with references to the speech transcript.
3. Go through the speech and find instances of the speaker's self-effacement. What is the likely impact upon this audience of such an apparently modest approach?

4. Describe and evaluate the level of language and style in this speech, taking into account its speaker, topic, audience, and occasion.
5. Analyze the communication function of humor in this speech. Do the comic moments "work" in terms of audience perception and the speech's purpose?
6. Assess the validity of the speaker's logic.
7. Describe the implied speaker in this transcript. What are his tone of voice and apparent attitudes toward the topic and the audience?
8. If you were in the audience for this speech, how would you judge its merits and demerits?

## HYPOTHETICAL SPEECH

Imagine that you are a business executive invited to speak to a high school social studies class on the subject of private capital investments. Your task, in twenty minutes, is to convince this young audience that individual investors are essential to a healthy capitalist system and that one need not be a professional or a large investor to enter that system. When selecting the information to be included in this speech and when choosing the examples, the language, and the basic approach you will take, consider carefully who your audience is and what they are likely to bring to this speech occasion. Do not limit your presentation to the typical image of a classroom lecture with you at the lectern and the students taking notes. Rather, be creative in inventing an approach likely to convey information and to persuade. The real measure of this speech's success is not your performance but the audience's response; the challenge is to present new ideas in a way most likely to be remembered.

## SUMMARY

The real communication value of any speech depends as much upon an audience's perception as upon a speaker's intention. In fact, effective speech communication *demands* a partnership in which both speaker and listener make investments and from which each shares the profits or suffers the losses. To recognize and utilize this inseparable linkage with an audience, a business speaker must, at a minimum, conduct some analysis of the identities of potential listeners.

No segment of the general population can be ruled out as the prospective audience for business speech. However, no single address is likely to speak with equal meaning and impact to all audiences. Because any listener brings to a speech certain predispositions likely to affect perception, a speaker must try to anticipate these by answering a wide range of important questions. An accurate audience profile includes (1) demographic information, (2) a description of the listeners' business context, (3) an assessment of prior knowledge and attitudes toward the speech topic, (4) consideration of a listener's relationship to the speaker and corporation represented, and (5) some survey of an audience's vested interests in the speech topic and its consequences. Without due consideration to each area of inquiry, a speaker must rely on a hit-or-miss strategy for communication. By means of a thorough and sensible audience analysis, a speaker should be able to lay out a broad common ground on which real engagement with the listener is possible.

This analysis phase of speech preparation probes the identity of a real audience apart from the actual speech event. One can also speak of an *implied audience* alive within the language, structure, and delivery of a public speech. That is, a speaker projects his or her knowledge of, attitude toward, and feelings about an audience by every choice of composition and performance. If these projections match the real interests and predispositions of an audience, communication dividends are paid. If, however, a speaker projects unreasonable expectations based on false assumptions about an audience, communication losses accrue. An implied audience is made manifest at every level of a speech but becomes particularly apparent in a speaker's selection of information, his or her word choices, and manner of delivery.

Underlying these critical concerns with audience analysis and projection is a basic principle of speech communication: audience perception is primarily temporal. Meaning accumulates over time; persuasion is affected by a sequence of small changes; perceptual movement is essential to discourse. If a speaker's goal is to elicit a certain response from the audience by the end of a speech, this can only be accomplished by mapping out a whole series of changes likely to lead the listener to a desired end. And that process of change depends fundamentally upon an understanding of where an audience begins. Without an accurate assessment of audience interests, attitudes, and knowledge, and without a tangible projection of these into the language of public speech, a speaker cannot hope to serve as a reliable guide to reasonable change. An efficient match between the real audience and that listener implied by a speech's expectations and assumptions is likely to yield real communication benefits to a speaker.

# 6

# The Audience: Listening and Viewing

This chapter and the next discuss and offer practice in various dimensions of audience perception. Here we shall be interested primarily in what an audience looks at and listens to during a speech event; in Chapter 7, we shall be more concerned with how an audience assesses validity in a speech text. In all of the discussions of audience perception, our dual objectives are (1) to become smarter consumers of business speech, while (2) increasing performance competence as business speakers. The two perspectives are linked intimately: one cannot achieve excellence in speech communication without first becoming expert in speech perception.

## MODES OF PERCEPTION

It might be assumed that since speech is an *oral* activity, audience response is based on *aural* perception. The simplicity of this view is appealing: a speaker speaks, and a listener listens. Unfortunately, the matched phenomena of speech and perception are not described adequately by this elementary equation. The problem is with a faulty premise in the if-clause. As we explored in Chapter 4, speech performance is not an exclusively oral activity; it includes a whole range of nonverbal behaviors complementing or contradicting the sound dimension of language. Similarly, speech audiences receive much more than acoustic signals; their perception is multidimensional. If a speaker is to anticipate and in some measure shape audience response, one must understand these various modes of perception.

At the most basic level, an audience receives information on three performance levels — language, voice, and visual image or movement. These cannot be separated easily or neatly because they are fused so tightly to one another in the perceived message of a speech. For the purposes of analysis, however, an artificial separation of these three aspects may be useful. Until an individual grasps that speech communication is more than mere words and that audience response may be provoked on several levels, the speaker labors under a delusion.

Let's be clear at the outset about what kinds of performance behaviors are included on each level of audience perception. *Language* consists of a speaker's word choices, grammar, syntax, sentence lengths, rhetorical development, logical arguments, and such structural markers as introduction and conclusion. Three later chapters will be devoted entirely to matters of language, organization, and persuasion in a speech text. Because of the special importance of introductions and conclusions to audience perception, these will be discussed in this chapter. All of the language features of speech communication are familiar and may come first to mind when one thinks of the activity. Indeed, you may have expected that our study would begin with language rather than leading to it as an ultimate topic. There is no doubt that a speaker's primary obligation is to the language level of communication: one is held accountable, first and foremost, for the words one speaks. The difficulty in giving exclusive attention to this aspect of preparation is that it ignores certain fundamentals of audience perception. An audience's attention is directed toward and away from language by other aspects of speech performance, often primary in the sequence of perceptions.

The *voice* dimension of communication consists of paralanguage of every description — tone, pitch, rhythm, rate, accent, emphasis, loudness, and quality. We have spoken of these aspects before, in terms of performance. It is important to note in this context that voice is also a critical feature of perception. From the speaker's viewpoint, voice (if well used) is a tool for underscoring meaning. From an audience perspective, voice provides cues and directives for attention as well as conditioning meaning. When experiencing another's speech, we rely on tone of voice to interpret attitude and commitment. We count on rhythm and pause to isolate key ideas and terms. We respond to vocal emphasis and inflection as memory aids. And we place some credence on the combination of all vocal characteristics as an indication of the speaker's personality, authority, and viewpoint. In speech communication the perception of language cannot be divorced from voice.[1] Words are uttered by a given speaker, and the quality of that utterance facilitates perception and helps to shape meaning for an audience. Good

---

[1] The argument is persuasive suggesting that reader perception of printed matter also depends upon implied voice. See the author's *Business Correspondence: Writer, Reader, and Text* (Englewood Cliffs, N.J.: Prentice-Hall, Inc., 1983) and *The Business Report: Writer, Reader, and Text* Englewood Cliffs, N.J.: Prentice-Hall, Inc., 1983).

listeners are particularly alert for any discrepancies between language and voice. Irony, sarcasm, real and false modesty, and some brands of humor are instances of meanings prescribed by a particular relationship between voice and language.

Audience perception also depends upon a *visual* level of communication. Everything that one sees in speech performance contributes to the specific meaning of a text and to the significance of the event as a whole (i.e., the context). Visual stimuli include the lighting, color, decor, and arrangement of a room or auditorium. They include, as well, the appearance, dress, grooming, gestures, mannerisms, expressions, and movements of a speaker. Observe carefully your own visual perceptions at a speech event, and notice how communication begins from the moment when you walk into a room. You look up and around, making observations of the environment and drawing conclusions about its corporate sponsor. The visual images of a speech environment (including the speaker's physical behavior and appearance) are linked to language and meaning in a listener's memory.

The listening and viewing modes of audience perception (including language, voice, and visual imagery) function in complementary ways. A keen audience member organizes the rich variety of perceptual cues into a system of checks and balances. Just as a good listener in everyday conversation withholds judgment, a competent speech audience accumulates ample perceptual data before drawing conclusions. Thus, for instance, if one walks into a room where a speech is to be given and finds the chairs arranged haphazardly, half of the ceiling lights on and half off, and the chalkboard still covered with the scribblings of a previous session, one may assume that the event has been poorly prepared. Reasonable caution, however, should not allow this audience member to blame the speaker for slipshod preparation. These visual stimuli, nevertheless, register at some level of perception. When the speaker appears, then, he or she will be seen to contradict the earlier negative impression or to confirm it. If that speaker arrives late and disheveled, the visual perceptions of an audience begin to form a pattern of meaning. They say something even before the speaker has uttered a word. Similarly, language and voice are used as checks on one another.

A speech audience scans the event for *patterns* of meaning, for perceptions that fit together and make sense. The perspiration on a speaker's brow matches the nervous hitch in his voice and the unstable wobble of his legs and prescribes a pattern of perceived meaning: this fellow is unsure of himself or his subject. Or, to cite a positive case, the impeccable appearance of a speaker becomes linked in audience perception to her confident stature and easy delivery—all forming a perceived pattern of authority.

When a member of an audience scans these modes of perception, he or she places certain observations in the foreground and others in the background. Just as accurate visual perception depends upon a figure-ground relationship to determine the size, texture, and other qualities of an object, speech perception demands a similar arrangement of perceptions. One word or behavior takes on enormous importance in the minds of an audience while another fades into the background or may not be noticed at all. A person leaves a speech event remembering only certain words, tones, and images, and memory is structured by patterns of linkage.

The lesson of this discussion for an apprentice speaker is the implied mandate that he or she take command of communication at every level possible. If a speaker can control the physical setting of a room and facilitate efficient listening and viewing for an audience, one should do so. Furthermore, a good speaker understands the variety of perceptions on which an audience will base meaning, and he or she tries to aid the formation of reliable patterns. Like a theater director who blocks action and movement to give dramatic focus where it belongs, a speaker should direct audience attention in an efficient and reliable way. Everything about a speech presentation should *point* the audience to where the speaker wants them to look and listen. All performance behavior (both visual and oral) should combine to place in the foreground of audience perception what the speaker wants most to communicate.

Implicit in this overview is the paramount importance of audience perception in speech communication. Ultimately, it matters less what a speaker intends to say or present; it matters more what an audience perceives. For example, a speaker may be perfectly sincere in his or her caring for an audience, but if his tone of voice is perceived as sarcastic or aloof, an audience will hear the opposite of what is intended, and communication will be distorted. Similarly, it does not matter that a speaker is nervous or has a headache; it only matters whether or not the audience can perceive the symptoms. This is to state the case quite strongly, though accurately, and the facts of audience perception offer to a public speaker both challenge and comfort. The challenge is to fashion one's intended message in such language, voice, and behavior that it may be received reliably and with memorable impact by an audience. The comfort is that audience perceptions can be predicted by the common sense observations of one's own consumer experience.

## THE FUNCTION OF HUMOR IN BUSINESS SPEECH

An underlying principle of performance in this discussion of audience perception is that a speaker should present a consistent pattern of signals. Verbal and nonverbal behaviors should complement each other in projecting a whole image. Language and voice should blend in the utterance of a single message. Such consistency assists audience perception by projecting an integrated pattern of meaning. One notable exception to this virtue of speech performance is the use of humor. Humor depends for its effect upon incongruity, a purposeful inconsistency on the speaker's part.

Comedy ranges all the way from physical farce (a pratfall or a pie in the face) to intellectual wit (a clever turn of phrase or a startling shift in perspective). Between these extremes fall all manner of jokes, puns, and anecdotes. Humor, regardless of its source or intention, depends upon incongruity for its effects — something that violates an expected pattern. Good comedy can provide a pleasant diversion in the midst of an otherwise somber speech; it can gain and focus audience attention; it can, on occasion, provide a clever structure for discourse as a whole. At its best, humor is a radical tool for persuasion: it can turn around a familiar situation by adopting a totally unexpected viewpoint and, thus, can teach an important lesson.

Consideration of humor belongs in a discussion of perception because a comic effect resides entirely with the audience. Something is deemed funny only by perception, not intention. And a speaker must be careful that an audience perceives humor where it is intended.

As a general rule, wit is preferable to jokes in business speech. Unless a speaker is a proven expert in telling jokes, there is great danger of a story falling flat and alienating an audience rather than winning support. Furthermore, jokes, unless well integrated into a text, often appear as awkward and unnecessary appendages to discourse, merely filling time without substance. Wit, on the other hand, offers several winning advantages to audience perception. A speaker's clever and imaginative use of language or an apt anecdote can teach and persuade while entertaining an audience. A proper blend of entertainment and instruction can be very effective in directing audience attention and eliciting a favorable response.

Two dangers should be considered when using a comic variable as part of a speech strategy. First, a speaker should ensure that his or her total communication (language, voice, and image) will facilitate proper interpretation by an audience. An ironic speech, for instance, in which a speaker really means the opposite of what is said, can be effective only if the irony is clearly perceived. If the tongue-in-cheek voice is *not* perceived, an audience may go away with the opposite message of that intended. In addition to monitoring all dimensions of comic perception, a speaker should be aware of the danger of inadvertent humor. If an audience perceives gross incongruities between levels of performance, these may become comic despite the speaker's serious intent.

Comedy can be an effective communication approach to an entire speech assignment or to an aspect of a subject. However, an astute speaker must realize that humor depends upon perception. What one person finds funny, another may not, just as the same circumstances can make one individual cry while another person remains unmoved. In the use of humor, like any other communication strategy, a speaker must make his or her choices with a proper view of audience perception.

## VISUAL AIDS

A public speaker communicates on several dimensions at the same time. A good speaker aims to engage the audience sensibly at each level, and one means of doing so is to employ visual aids. By focusing attention on some visual display of information, a speaker controls perception and augments the channels of communication with an audience. There are many aids available to the speaker who prepares ahead and who can anticipate the needs of audience perception. These devices fall into five basic groups.

The first kind of visual aid, often the most useful, are *graphics* — tables, graphs, charts, diagrams, and photos. These provide a visible display of numbers and percentages, financial and market trends, budgets and expenditures, manufacturing goals and productivity. Well-designed graphics can clarify an otherwise complex discussion and can cause an audience to remember figures and data that may escape when explained through language alone.

A second category of visual aids includes *slides and films*. When a speech presents primarily visual information, these two media can be very effective in engaging an audience. Slides stand in the foreground of sense perception, and the speaker serves as narrator or commentator in the background of audience attention. A film interrupts speech. It can, nonetheless, punctuate a verbal presentation with documentary impact. A speaker considering the use of slides or film must determine the relative merits of a picture versus language in presenting certain information to an audience.

The third category of visual aid, popular in educational settings, is the printed *handout*. It can take several forms—an outline of the speaker's presentation, a list of references, quotations, or bibliography, a series of examples or hypotheticals, or an exercise sheet for audience participation and response. A handout gives the listener something tangible to take away from the speech event; if well conceived, it can document the communication for future reference. It can also assist the audience during a speech to follow its progress by eye as well as ear.

The *chalkboard* or writing pad are also potential aids to a speaker. Like graphics and handouts, the use of these devices supplies visual support to verbal communication. The distinctive feature of this type of aid is its apparent spontaneity. The graphic is being produced on the spot as opposed to the prior production of a printed display. Interestingly, writing on the chalkboard or pad not only serves visual communication; it also punctuates the rhythm of verbal discourse. As a professor orchestrates a lecture by movement to and from the chalkboard, the business speaker can direct audience attention by a sensible use of these instruments.

A final category of visual aid is *props*. Most speeches of demonstration demand them; many other speeches may benefit by their use. As with the other aids, props focus attention. Sight reinforces hearing, and information is exchanged through two senses simultaneously.

Regardless of the kind of aid used, a speaker should follow five guidelines in choosing visual strategies of communication:

1. The visual aid must present complete and accurate information. This obligation entails valid perspective, descriptive titles and headings, and a proper scale of measurement.
2. The aid must be appropriate to the subject and to the audience. Its design must allow for all dimensions of a subject's complexity; the aid must facilitate the understanding of a particular audience.
3. Aids should be as simple as possible in their visual design. If the graphic features are too complicated, the aid is likely to distract an audience rather than to point attention to a speaker's focus.
4. Any graphic display, including chalkboard or writing pad, must be of sufficient size to be seen easily by all members of an audience.
5. Graphic design and production should meet professional aesthetic standards. Just as the typing and printing of a letter or report reflect on their writer, the design and production of visual aids are perceived to represent a speaker. Whether or not a speaker has actually made the visual aid, his or her use of it makes one accountable for its clarity, design, and accuracy.

## INTRODUCTIONS AND CONCLUSIONS

Our interest throughout this chapter has been in modes of perception. An audience not only pays heed to language but to voice and image, as well. This means that a speaker must be aware of his or her total communicative behavior and must seek to bring each performance signal into line with an overall strategy. Everything that a speaker says and does directs audience attention, whether or not the speaker intends focus to go to the point perceived. Two parts of any speech are essential to this focusing process — the introduction and the conclusion.

In later discussions of specific speech types, we shall discuss appropriate beginnings and endings for each category. The purpose in addressing the topic here is to see the usefulness of these speech parts in shaping accurate audience perception. There are many good ways to introduce a speech — with a question, with a quotation, with an anecdote, or with a straightforward exposition of data. There are as many effective ways of closing — with a summary, with a call for action, with a question demanding audience response, or with a compelling example in support of the speaker's viewpoint. There are no strict formulas for proper introductions and conclusions. There are only guidelines to assist the speaker in choosing a suitable approach.

A good introduction serves three essential functions. First, it presents clearly and forcefully the persona of a speaker. From the moment that an individual assumes the rostrum and utters the first word, audience perceptions begin adding up to judgment. Therefore an introduction must serve to establish the speaker's presence and authority. Second, a good introduction must gain and focus the audience's attention on a speaker's intended message. The topic and its scope must be presented clearly, with definitions of any problematic terms or ideas. Perhaps most importantly, an introduction must establish in the minds of audience members an accurate expectation of what is to come. It must anticipate the speech's structure as a whole and guide the listener easily into the main body of discourse. Hence, an introduction serves all three components of a speech act — speaker, audience, and text.

A good conclusion, too, addresses the needs of each speech participant. A speaker must exit leaving a memorable impression of his or her credibility. The audience must be left with a whole pattern of related perceptions by which memory may be solidified and an appropriate response evoked. A speech text itself must reach closure in its logical development and its structural (or aesthetic) shape.

As with all other aspects of speech performance, the merits of an introduction and a conclusion can only be measured by the experience of an audience. Ultimately, both speaker and text must be held accountable to the listener. And a close look at how the audience perceives indicates a dual reliance upon the ear and the eye as complementary channels of communication. Speech perception changes and accumulates over time as patterns of meaning evolve from the checks and balances of sight and sound. A careful speaker, intent upon real engagement with an audience, must blend all performance behaviors into a unified strategy of effective communication.

## EXERCISES

**A**   It is popularly accepted, and research confirms, that speech audiences trust nonverbal signals more than verbal messages in situations when the two conflict. For example, if an individual accused of fraud addresses an audience in self-defense and perspires profusely while stammering through the denial, these visual and vocal signals will contradict language. An audience is more likely to believe the nonverbal than the verbal behavior; or, at least, the nonverbal behavior is likely to cast doubt on the veracity of speech.

Make a list of specific *visual* cues that you look for to test a speaker's preparedness and confidence.

1.
2.
3.
4.
5.

Make a list of specific *visual* cues that you look for to test a speaker's truthfulness.

1.
2.
3.
4.
5.

Make a list of specific *visual* and *vocal* cues that you perceive to indicate an ironic or teasing approach to a speech subject.

1.
2.
3.
4.
5.

**B**   There are several acceptable ways to deliver a business speech — from a complete manuscript, from an outline, from notes, or without any script. Speculate upon the differences in perception that may result from the following descriptions of speech performance.

1. A speaker stands up to lead a one-hour seminar without any notes. What is your first expectation of communication competence?

2. A speaker delivers a three-minute sales promotion reading every word verbatim from a typed manuscript. What conclusions are you likely to draw from this performance choice?

3. A speaker distributes printed outlines of his address and then announces that he or she will not follow the document's sequence. What judgments are you likely to attach to this approach?

4. Three individuals speak on the same program of a business conference. The audience numbers two hundred. The first speaker stands behind a lectern and delivers his or her address from notes, establishing eye contact and an open relationship with the audience. The second speaker reads his or her address from a printed manuscript in a clear voice. The third speaker sits on the edge of the platform and chats with the audience without notes or printed outline. From these minimal descriptions, what perceptions are you likely to attach to each speaker's approach?

**C** Ask each member of the class to write up a favorite joke or comic anecdote. As a group, then analyze samples by answering the following questions:

1. What is the instance of incongruity in this joke?
2. How does the sequence of information or events in the joke help to control audience perception?
3. What performance behaviors (qualities of voice or movement) does the joke demand for maximum comic effect?
4. Imagine a speech situation in which the joke would be appropriate and one in which the same joke would be inappropriate. What variables in a speech context determine appropriateness?
5. Besides the comic value of the joke, what other judgments of the speaker might an audience make in response to the joke?

**D** Read each of the following speech scenarios, and write a one-paragraph *introduction* for each. Remember that your introduction should gain and focus audience attention while introducing the speech's subject.

1. You are a company president addressing all employees to announce a policy of no pay raises during the upcoming year because of profit losses during the current year.

2. You are a company president addressing all employees to announce an across-the-board 10 percent pay increase in recognition of increased corporate profits.

3. You are a company president addressing all employees to announce your early retirement and promotion to chairperson of the board.

4. You are a company president addressing all employees to announce your decision to leave and to accept a post in government service.

5. You are a company president addressing all employees to announce your resignation for reasons of ill health.

## SAMPLE SPEECH

Here is a speech delivered by a hospital's chief resident of family practice physicians to a class of seniors in high school. The subject, as will become clear, is cigarette smoking. The speaker's perspective is, perhaps, less apparent. As you evaluate the merits and demerits of this speech, put yourself in the position of a high school audience.

---

I've been invited by your school's administration to address you today on the subject of cigarette smoking—a topic with which most of you were perfectly familiar in the seventh grade and which probably bores you to death by now. As a physician, I too am bored by the topic having read a good deal about it, conducted research, and treated many patients with physical ailments associated in one way or another with smoking. Despite our similar attitudes toward today's subject, I'll request that you listen carefully. In exchange for your attention, I shall promise to be brief.

The reason why I am here and why I occasionally speak to other groups is to convince the nonsmokers in the audience to begin the habit, to encourage the casual smokers among you to take their behavior more seriously, and to applaud the chain smokers for their social responsibility. Statistics indicate that only 40 percent of you smoke more than one pack of cigarettes each day, and I am here to do my part in increasing that percentage.

Think for a minute about the many benefits of smoking, and if you'll withhold judgment till the end of my talk, I think you'll be persuaded.

I do not make my appeal for more young people to smoke on a personal basis. I do not claim that cigarettes will make you better looking, more socially acceptable, or that smoking will help you relax. You are too smart and sophisticated to buy such tired arguments.

My appeal is to your altruism. I want you to consider others more than yourselves, to put the good of society above individual welfare. The revolution that I advocate, if it is to succeed, must begin with young people like yourselves; my generation with its paltry 36 percent of smokers has already dropped the ball.

Increased smoking would create a ripple effect of economic prosperity throughout our depressed society. First, think of the tobacco growers, cigarette manufacturers, wholesalers, and retailers. Increased sales would benefit each group, with the prospects of even greater employment in the tobacco industries. But that's just the beginning.

With more cigarette sales, the government would not need to support the tobacco industry as it does now, and that money could be freed for other uses. Of course, increased sales would also swell government coffers with additional tax revenues.

Are you with me so far?

Think now about the long-range benefits of every young American forming the habit in his or her teens of smoking three or four packs per day. The results would be spectacular. First, the life expectancy of Americans would decline dramatically. Within two or three generations, we would have few citizens in their seventies and no octogenarians. Think of the social security savings.

Men and women would be forced into early retirement at age fifty by emphysema, cancers of all descriptions, and cardiovascular fatigue. This would open up the job market for younger people.

The increased incidence of prolonged and painful illness in our society would benefit doctors, hospitals, drug companies, and the insurance business.

While the benefits of this smoking revolution are primarily economic, there are social advantages, too. With a large percentage of our adult population in constant pain and distress, short of breath, hair falling out, without appetites, and unable to digest what food they eat, psychoses of unimagined variety would develop, thus filling churches and the offices of psychiatrists with individuals desperate to become well-adjusted to their fatal conditions. We would experience less misunderstanding between generations of Americans because young children, for the most part, would not know their grandparents — at least, not for long.

Now, some of you are probably saying, "This is too good to be true." You're skeptical of my campaign promises. Let me assure you that I am running for no office, that medical research is unequivocal in supporting the very results I've suggested for increased smoking. If enough of you start smoking enough cigarettes soon enough, by age forty, the majority of this audience will be well on your ways to terminal cancer, the most painful and unpleasant death known to mankind. And if enough of you smoke, even those few holdouts will have a good chance of contracting the disease just from associating with the sensible smokers.

Think about it, and see if you don't agree with me. And, if my arguments have not convinced you, consider the alternative. Consider what kind of society this would be if no one smoked. I'm sure you'll see the light.

Thank you.

---

This speech is an example of what critic Wayne Booth calls "stable irony." The speaker treats his subject tongue-in-cheek from beginning to end. He means just the opposite of what he says and signals that intended message in several ways, exaggeration foremost among them. The delivery of this kind of speech demands an apparent seriousness throughout. If the speaker is seen to enjoy his or her own humor, the audience is less likely to enter into the rhetorical ruse. On the other hand, if the incongruity between behavior and intention is maintained on all levels of delivery, audience perception is enriched on both a comic and a serious dimension.

## DISCUSSION QUESTIONS

1. State the speaker's purpose in this speech.
2. At what precise point in the speech did you become aware of its ironic approach?

3. Analyze how this speech and its delivery controls audience perception through language, voice, and image.
4. If you were in the high school audience for this speech, how would you rate its communication effectiveness? What are the communication advantages and disadvantages of this communication strategy?
5. What difference in perception would accrue if the audience for this speech were sixth graders? Eighth graders? Seniors in college? A senior citizens group?
6. Read an excellent example of stable irony in Jonathan Swift's "A Modest Proposal." Discuss the possible uses of this communication strategy in business speech.

## HYPOTHETICAL SPEECH

Create a ten-minute speech in which you articulate and defend the "ideal relationship between business institutions and institutions of higher education." This is not an invitation to recite platitudes or to pay lip service to some inherited viewpoint. The speech represents a verbal "position paper" for which you must forge a specific perspective and then convince the audience of its validity. In analyzing this speech topic, consider the following questions:

1. To what extent, if any, should a college or a university education be viewed as corporate training?
2. To what extent, if any, should university research serve commercial or corporate ends?
3. To what extent, if any, should corporations subsidize schools or students?

You may limit the subject in whatever ways serve you best, provided the subject's scope is made clear in your introduction. Your viewpoint toward this complicated (and controversial) topic is, in itself, important; your presentation of that viewpoint through language, voice, and visual imagery is critical to the audience's understanding.

## SUMMARY

Speech perception includes all communicative signals received through the eye and the ear. The easy equation that speech is an *oral* activity and perception is an *aural* response deceives by its very simplicity. Both a speaker's performance and an audience's response depend upon several levels of speech communication. A business speaker cannot achieve excellence at his or her task without first becoming expert in the role of self-aware audience member.

Three modes of perception describe the basic means by which audiences receive information—language, voice, and image. *Language* consists of a speaker's word choices, grammar, syntax, sentence lengths, rhetorical development, logical arguments, and such structural markers as introduction and conclusion. *Voice* includes paralanguage of all descriptions—tone, pitch, rhythm, rate, accent, emphasis, loudness, and quality.

*Image* refers to every visual feature (static and mobile) of a speech presentation. This communication level includes environmental factors (e.g., lighting, color, decor, and room arrangement) and performance variables (e.g., appearance, gestures, mannerisms, and movements). The listening and viewing modes of audience perception function in complementary ways, as checks and balances. Perceptual data collected on each level of speech communication must fit into a reliable pattern of meaning for an audience. When this pattern matches the speaker's intention, the speech achieves communication success. Because such success depends ultimately upon audience perception, a speaker must be aware of every facet of performance behavior (language, voice, and image) and must calculate the likely impact of each upon the audience's attention and perceived meaning.

Humor can serve as an effective communication strategy in business speech. Its essential incongruity can startle, amuse, and teach. The danger of humor is that it may be perceived in a way other than that intended by a speaker. As a general rule, wit pays higher communication dividends than do jokes, and the use of any comic device must be based upon some reliable prediction and control of audience perception.

To facilitate communication at every level, a business speaker may choose from a wide inventory of visual aids. These include graphics, slides or films, handouts, a chalkboard or writing pad, and props. One must take care in the use of any visual aid that it be accurate, appropriate, simple in design, sufficient in size, and professionally produced.

This chapter's final topic of audience perception includes speech introductions and conclusions. While there are many effective approaches to these speech parts, a good introduction and a good conclusion must serve all three communication components—speaker, audience, and text. Each must present clearly and forcefully the persona of a speaker; each must focus audience attention and help to shape patterns of perception; each must contribute to the sensible structure of a speech text.

# 7

# The Audience: Assessment and Response

Audience perception includes both description and evaluation. One wants to know both what is there in a speech *and* what it's worth. The audience for a business presentation first must understand what is being said and *then* must determine whether the speaker's position has merit and demands action. Our interest in the previous chapter was primarily descriptive: what does an audience look at and listen to in a speech event? Our interest now is in evaluation: how does a speech audience assess merit and make response? Specifically, one offers three kinds of judgment, whether consciously or unconsciously, when assessing speech. These are described by the chapter's three headings—*speaker* credibility, *textual* validity, and *audience* reliability.

## SPEAKER CREDIBILITY

When one listens to a speech and decides whether or not to believe it and to act upon its appeal, a major variable of one's response is the speaker's credibility. The common sense connection between rhetorical validity and speaker credibility is apparent in the gossip's caution ("Just consider the source . . .") and in the newscaster's assurance ("According to a reliable source . . . "). Our perception of information is conditioned by the identity, believability, and authority of the speaker. For this reason, the first sensible response to hearing a rumor, for instance, is to ask, "From *whom* did you hear this story?" One decides whether or not to act on the information, to pass it along, or simply to ignore it partly on the basis of source credibility. Examples exist in business speech of audiences accepting bad logic from a speaker deemed highly credible and of audiences rejecting the perfectly sensible argument of a speaker considered dubious in his or her credentials.

In trying to persuade an audience of anything (e.g., to adopt a policy, to learn a procedure, or to buy a product), speakers must be concerned with their perceived credibility. Competent listeners are right to link their assessment and response, in part, to the speaker's persona. Workaday examples of this phenomenon are numerous:

> "I don't know what Fitzsimmons has in mind, but if it's her idea you can bank on its working."

Or, to take a negative example,

> "No matter what, I'll never vote for one of William's plans. Experience has taught me that they're full of hidden traps."

Investors, too, make decisions based upon the perceived credibility of an individual or a corporation, often as much as upon the merits of a given prospectus. It would be useless to argue whether judgments represented by such arguments are valid or good. Speaker credibility is an inevitable part of audience perception and must be taken into account when one chooses a communication strategy.

When conferring credibility upon a speaker, speech audiences ask four basic questions:

1. What is the general reputation of this speaker, as gleaned from prior contact or word-of-mouth opinion?
2. How much does the speaker know about the subject from both personal experience and research?
3. With what other authorities can I associate this speaker's viewpoint?
4. What are the speaker's attitudes toward this particular speech occasion and its audience?

These questions survey a speaker's reputation, knowledge, authority, and attitude. An audience's answers to these questions add up to an assessment of believability. Judgments based upon such answers elicit trust or skepticism; they help to control or to divert attention; they condition audience response. Often, neither the questions nor their answers are articulated consciously in the mind of an audience member. They serve as a kind of subtext to communication suffusing language, voice, and image.

A good speaker, devoted to effective communication, can do something positive about each of these questions of credibility. Establishing a reputation of trustworthiness is the theme of any successful business career. It pays dividends in all phases of a commercial operation, and it yields high returns in both interpersonal and public communication. The business person who comes to a speech event preceded by this expectation of reliability begins the task of communication with a real advantage. Conversely, a speaker burdened by the reputation of being untrustworthy labors against an incredible obstacle in winning audience attention and acceptance. An assessment of trustworthiness is no simple judgment. It includes, at a minimum, an expectation of honesty, fairness, a measure of objectivity, and an assurance that the speaker has done his or her homework—has investigated a subject and determined a viewpoint with thorough study and reasoned analysis. Such a reputation cannot be won by any shortcuts or by coercion. It is, quite literally, the work of a lifetime and, if successful, can open wide channels of communication with ever larger constituencies.

The second reasonable question that an audience asks about credibility has to do with the speaker's knowledge of a subject. We tend to trust most those individuals who speak from personal experience; hence, one does well to emphasize any first-hand contact he or she has had with a topic. When personal experience is not available or does not apply, an audience can be assured of the speaker's knowledge only by the record of his or her research and analysis. One can display this preparation not only by reporting findings and conclusions but, more importantly, by tracing in a speech the process of one's research and logical deductions. If members of an audience can follow the speaker's step-by-step processes of data collection and reasoning, they are more likely to follow and endorse the speaker's conclusions.

A speaker gains credibility in response to the third question of audience perception by associating himself or herself with highly credible authorities. This is a complicated matter involving a transfer of qualities from one person or group to another. We are familiar with this approach to gaining audience approval through television commercial campaigns linking products or services to celebrity and linking attractiveness of the celebrity to the product. The same principle applies when a speaker quotes some authority in support of a speech premise. One hopes to bolster the credibility of an argument by the evidence of another's reasoning or experience *and* by the reputation of the other's name and authority. In selecting all outside references in support of a speech, one must question source credibility just as an audience assesses speaker credibility. And this kind of judgment applies to every aspect of the quoted material—its author, date, and publication.

An assessment of the speaker's attitudes toward a subject and an audience (the fourth question) is, perhaps, the most problematic and, in some ways, the most fundamental variable of perception. If members of an audience are to invest their trust in a speaker, they must *feel* that speaker's genuine interest in the topic and in their response. As with all other dimensions of a speech event, the only true measurement of effectiveness can be made by audience perception, not by the speaker's intention. Thus, it is not enough for a speaker to be excited about a topic and to be genuinely interested in the audience's response. These attitudes must *show* in preparation and delivery. They have to be available in order to be perceived. All questions of speaker attitude really come down to one issue: is he or she devoted fully to the goal of communication? Without deep interests in both a subject and an audience, and without a clear projection of these commitments, no speaker commands a listener's trust or attention.

Assessment and response, then, begin with an audience's judgment of the speaker — his or her reputation, knowledge, associations, and attitudes. But a competent speech audience cannot rely only upon these criteria of evaluation because the speech transaction does not depend solely upon a speaker. It depends, as well, upon the text and the audience.

When discussing speaker credibility, we looked back to earlier chapters devoted to performance. In introducing aspects of a text, we look forward to the succeeding three chapters, which are devoted to that topic. It is important here to bring together all components of a speech transaction because reliable audience response demands an understanding of each dimension.

## TEXTUAL VALIDITY

The text includes all of a speech's language — its vocabulary, syntax, and organization. As we shall see in subsequent discussions, a text (when considered carefully) represents a miniature replica of the relationship between speaker and audience. Into a speech's language, style, and structure are projected images of the speaker and expectations of the listener. These two projections form an implied relationship by which communication is either enhanced or impeded. When an audience judges the merits of a speech text, whether through conscious deliberation or unconscious instinct, they ask three basic questions.

1. Do the content and language of a speech reflect thorough preparation and complete analysis?
2. Does the speech's pattern of organization establish a clear and memorable structure?
3. Are the speaker's appeals for action and response based upon reasonable expectations of the listener?

Note that these levels of evaluation *within* a text correspond to criteria for judgment *outside* the text.

An answer to the first question requires an audience's analysis linking language to speaker. One wants to know whether the selection of information in a speech, its level of vocabulary, and its other stylistic features represent a reliable speaker and his or her accurate assumptions about an audience. An answer to the second question is based upon what we earlier termed spatial perception. If an audience is to respond positively to a speech, their attention must be held moment by moment, and their perceptions must accumulate over time into a memorable pattern of meaning. A good speaker not only makes sense when at the lectern; he or she provides a solid structure by which the speech may still make sense after the event. A speech is unlikely to prompt positive action from the audience who cannot remember its argument and reconstruct its development. The third question asks whether a speech's appeals are reasonable and fair. To be judged effective, a speech text must warrant the call for action that it makes. A speaker cannot expect a change of opinion without giving adequate reasons to warrant the expectation. A speaker cannot expect a purchase without convincing the audience by adequate evidence of their need to purchase, of the advantages in purchasing, and of their ability to purchase. Furthermore, all appeals, as we shall see, must be based upon a respect for the audience's freedom of choice. The coercion of an undeserved response through deception, flattery, illogic, emotion, threats, or implied bribes falls outside any legitimate definition of human commmunication and outside any profitable prescription for business efficiency.

## AUDIENCE RELIABILITY

Audiences base their assessment and response to speech presentations upon judgments of the speaker and upon evaluations of his or her text. Too many audiences stop at this point. They neglect to take into account the reliability of their own listening and viewing — of their own perceptions. They may ignore particular ways in which their vested interests, prior knowledge, and prejudices may affect perception. While a speaker has little control over this aspect of the communication process, one is well advised to consider it for the sake of becoming a better (more self-aware) consumer of business speech.

To test your own reliability as an audience member for a particular speech, ask three questions.

1. What prior knowledge and expertise do I possess regarding the speech topic?
2. What vested interests do I have regarding the speaker's viewpoint and appeal?
3. How well prepared am I to watch and listen with real attention and to retain the speech's message for continuing deliberation?

No one can answer these questions except the individual audience member, and too few speech audiences practice self-criticism. They assume naïvely (and wrongly) that communication is the sole responsibility of a speaker and that audience perception is a passive and neutral phenomenon. It is neither.

The reason one must measure one's own knowledge and expertise (the first question) is that these will influence a listener's assessment of speech competence. The more background information that one brings to a given topic, the more likely one is to make fine discriminations in judging a speaker's presentation. If, however, an audience member does not know the meanings of important words in a speech or the identities of the authorities quoted, such ignorance disqualifies much of this person's judgment. Accurate assessment without adequate knowledge is impossible. An outside critic might blame the speaker for not analyzing his or her audience properly in such a case, but audiences, too, should take the responsibility, whenever possible, to prepare themselves for accurate speech perception.

The second question deals with an audience member's vested interest in the topic and is a particularly important consideration in business speech. Vested interest may be defined as the listener's personal or corporate stake in a given perspective. If such interest is high, it can distort perception by creating insurmountable barriers. For example, if an audience member has just converted his or her industrial plant to coal power and hears a speaker advocate stricter government control of sulphurous emissions, the listener's vested interest may inhibit objective perception. When prejudices of any kind prevent an audience from listening fairly and judging objectively, these preconceived ideas distort perception and disqualify assessment. Again, a smart speaker might anticipate an audience's vested interests and deal with them directly. But listeners share the responsibility of minimizing the distorting effect of vested interests upon their perception of a speech.

The third question, preparedness to listen, asks simply that an audience member survey his or her readiness for a given speech event. If one is to assess fairly and to respond fully to the speaker, one must be ready to attend completely to multiple messages. This means, at a minimum, that an audience member must clear his or her mind of distractions, must sit where neither sight nor sound are inhibited, and must ask questions and demand clarifications whenever the opportunities for dialogue exist. A good audience member makes mental and written notes and is ready for reasoned discussion on any point of a speaker's logic or appeal.

The assessment and response of an audience to business speech depends, then, upon three levels of judgment. An audience member must evaluate the speaker's performance and persona, the merits and demerits of a text, and one's own reliability as a perceptive and active participant in speech communication.

## EXERCISES

**A**  Think about the credibility of speakers in relation to specific business topics and viewpoints. Read the following short descriptions of subject areas, and fill in the blank columns with the names of a highly credible speaker in the public eye and one with little or no credibility to address the given topic.

| Topic and Viewpoint | Speaker with High Credibility | Speaker with Low Credibility |
|---|---|---|
| Defense of American labor unions | | |
| Opposition to foreign trade quotas | | |
| Defense of private mineral development of federal lands | | |
| Opposition to tight federal money controls | | |

Defense of strict
compliance with federal
clean air and water
standards


Opposition to increased
development of commercial
nuclear power

**B**   Consider the source credibility for quotations within a business speech. List the names of ten national periodicals (newspapers, magazines, or journals) with recognizable authority (high credibility) in the coverage of industrial, business, and financial matters.

1. _____
2. _____
3. _____
4. _____
5. _____
6. _____
7. _____
8. _____
9. _____
10. _____

List the names of five popular magazines or journals with low credibility for their coverage of business news.

1. _____
2. _____
3. _____
4. _____
5. _____

**C**   Read the following speech excerpts, and evaluate their logical validity. If the argument is based upon a fallacy of reasoning, identify the error.

1. Our company's decline in market share began last year in the very quarter that Everett Mathias became our president. Now, with four straight quarters of decline under Mr. Mathias's leadership, a solution to this problem should be obvious.

2. Ninety-nine percent of all doctors surveyed indicated a preference for (brand name) aspirin for relief of minor headaches.

3. The company is instituting a four-day work week for a trial period of six months. Alternate schedules are available so that either Monday, Wednesday, or Friday may be taken off, based on the hope that such a flexible arrangement will meet the greatest number of employee time needs.

4. Whereas international competition for product markets has been useful and profitable in the past, rapid change in the worldwide economy makes cooperation the mandate for future international trade.

5. Mr. Frances has shown his new fancy computer readouts and his pretty market projections based on so-called scientific evidence. I'm here to tell you that this company was built on old-fashioned horse sense, not computers. What was good enough for my father is good enough for me and will be good enough to guide this company when Mr. Frances's computers have gone the way of the wringer washing machine.

6. Every one of our competitors is starting a rebate program. We should, too.

7. Because weapons and military technology represent the largest share of American exports, doesn't it make sense to establish some formal ties between the Departments of Commerce and Defense?

**D** Examine your own prejudices, and explore your reliability as an audience for business speech by answering the following questions.

1. By what means, if any, should a goverment protect its businesses from foreign competition?

2. What important differences, if any, do you perceive between the attitudes of American labor today and those of twenty years ago?

3. To what constituency is a business executive most accountable — shareholders? employees? consumers? government? other?

4. Are there other reliable standards for measuring business success than profitability?

5. Is there an average age range beyond which executive performance begins to decline?

6. Should business hiring and promotion policies be based upon any criteria other than personal credentials and seniority (e.g., minority status)?

7. What examples of personal appearance, if any, would you cite as violating professional decorum and as being, thus, unacceptable for a business speaker?

8. In what circumstances, if any, should a business executive or a union official endorse a political candidate or legislative issue?

9. What is the proper role, if any, of industry lobbies in Washington?

10. What is the maximum length (in minutes) of a speech before audience attention begins to diminish?

Conduct a personal audit of your own reliability as an audience for business speech. What other prejudices, attitudes, and vested interests than those identified above do you possess that may become obstacles to proper perception or reliable evaluation of business speech?

## SAMPLE SPEECH

Here is the transcript of a speech delivered by Dr. Donald MacDonald, while serving as an Air Force Staff Information Officer in 1965 in Japan, to a joint meeting of the Rotary Club and the Commerce Association. Although the speech context was military rather than commercial, there are clear parallels between this speaker's role as spokesman for a larger constituency and that of a business representative speaking on behalf of a corporation. The speech is actually an introduction to a film, as will become clear. When reading the transcript, put yourself in the mind of the Japanese audience and observe dimensions of your assessment and response. The speech was originally delivered in Japanese, and this transcript is a translation.

Mr. President, friends. When Mito Sensei asked me to speak here he made one condition. It was that I must not talk about Misawa Air Base. That's fair enough, and if I mention the base except in passing, I'll volunteer a thousand yen for the smile box.

There are so many things that we of America and you of Japan have to say to each other. Just about twenty years ago — one generation of men — we ended a bitter war. In the years since then your nation and ours have shown the most amazing progress in the history of the world. In doing so, we have shined the light of understanding on our own histories and our own cultures.

When I was a small boy, I was afraid of the dark. I couldn't see what was there; I couldn't understand the darkness. But when I was in the light, and with my family and friends, it was a very happy life. I think we are like that as nations and races. We fear what we do not understand.

In my youth, most of the people around my home were much like me. But as I grew older, I found that there were strange and different people in the world. At first, the strangeness and differences were uncomfortable. I did not understand them, and in a sense I suppose they caused fear. Then I made a startling discovery.

Every Italian boy, or Polish girl, or Negro or German or Swede in my town was like me in more ways than he was different. When a Polish girl is hurt she runs to her mother for comfort. When a Negro boy is bewildered by the cruelty of strangers, he looks to his father for support and understanding. And so it was with all of us.

Finally, I came to Japan, just about four years ago. My wife and daughter soon arrived, and alone or together we met and made friends with Japanese people from every walk of life.

Now, I wish I could say that we understand everything about Japan and the Japanese people. But that is not true. We are the product of a very different way of thinking, which has its roots in the Christian and Jewish religions. You, on the other hand, are the products of Buddhism and Shinto. The only way for one of us to understand the other system completely, I suppose, is to be born and raised in the other society.

Still, there are many things that we can do to let a little light into the darkness of misunderstanding and ignorance. Let me tell you the picture that a small child from America used to have about the Orient. We believed that an oriental person never really smiles or, if he does, it's only to hide some evil purpose. We believed that everywhere you turned there would be an opium den full of men and women ready to commit any crime. We believed that the things manufactured in the Orient were shoddy copies of American goods.

On the other hand, in talking with Japanese people, I have found that you had ready-made impressions of Americans before most of you had ever seen one. We were all gangsters, carrying machine guns, chewing gum, and involved in all sorts of crimes. Our women all wore scandalous dresses and were libertines. The rest of us were cattle rustlers or red-faced Indians, ready to shoot or scalp any stranger at sight.

Then I came to Japan. Then my family and I began to see the light. And what did we see? A hard-working people that has produced the most modern manufacturing factory in the world. A nation of people filled with imagination that has revolutionized the photographic and electronics industries. A happy, laughing people that loves nothing more than a party, a picnic, and a tour to some scenic spot. A nation of people that displays an amazing tenderness toward its beautiful children. And a land where education is a prize to be worked for. We have also seen the gang boys, the terrible traffic jams in Tokyo, the occasional poverty, and the split personality of young people trying to combine the best of this modern, neon-lighted world with the traditional values that have made Japan a great nation.

You have seen that we are not all gangsters. You have seen that most of our wives are moral. You have seen that not quite all of us are cowboys or Indians. And you may have learned that we, too, believe in the value of education for ourselves and our children.

By these contacts we cast light on what was once darkness. As we light the way, the fears and doubts of misunderstanding fly away.

There is much more to do, for many of us have only begun to believe — and understanding does not necessarily bring belief — that bringing more light is a good thing.

The problem is not only between Japan and the United States. It is between all nations and peoples. And nations have taken many roads to increase understanding. In a moment I will ask you to look at a motion picture that shows an American city that represents how the people of many nations have all become Americans — New York. I hope you enjoy it, think about it, and develop ideas of your own.

From me and my family, I say only this. We have fallen in love with all of you, your ways, your sense of beauty, and your ideals of peace. We will never forget you. I hope you will not forget us.

---

Analysis of this speech is doubly complicated by its translation from another language and by the passage of time since its delivery. Much has changed in the respective cultural perceptions of Japan and the United States. Yet, the speech's basic thesis, that increased understanding of cultural differences and similarities is educational, and therefore good, remains a viable position. The diplomatic aim of this speaker is not unique to his military assignment or to the specific intercultural context. Business representatives often find themselves on diplomatic missions when making public presentations. The *world* of business, while a cliché, describes an important perception: business *is* a place, a culture. Public communication by representatives of that world to audiences of other (nonbusiness) cultures is an exercise in diplomacy.

## DISCUSSION QUESTIONS

1. What is the communication impact of the fact that this speech is delivered in Japanese rather than through an interpreter? Can you detect evidence in the text's language, content, or structure that would indicate its composition and delivery in a foreign

tongue? What specific differences in audience perception, assessment, and response would result if the speech were delivered through an interpreter?

2. Go back through the text and cite all examples of the speaker's recognition of Japanese culture. Discuss the communication impact of each example. Start by speculating upon the communication merits and demerits in the introductory reference to a "smile box."

3. In what specific ways does this speech *date* itself? For each example of a dated reference, vocabulary choice, or perspective, discuss the effect of time upon changing perception. That is, how would such references have been received at the date of delivery and how would they be perceived if stated in the same language today?

4. Discuss the communication impact of the light and dark images in this speech.

5. Discuss the appropriateness of the child images throughout the speech. What are the advantages in using such imagery in this context for the speaker's apparent purpose? Are there any disadvantages to this communication choice?

6. Discuss equivalent situations in business communication when a speaker may be called upon to "shine a light of understanding" upon cultural differences and fears.

## HYPOTHETICAL SPEECH

As a group, conduct a sales conference extending over at least two class sessions. Schedule a four-minute presentation for each student to make a promotional speech. You are to introduce and try to sell a new product or service. Imagine that your audience consists of prospective investors who, if persuaded by your presentation, will supply the necessary capital for you to begin a manufacturing or service business. For this assignment, you must invent the product prototype or service pilot. Adopt whatever mode of delivery seems best suited to the subject and the audience. Be sure to use your full time without exceeding the four-minute limit. Consider the value of visual aids to this kind of presentation. And devise your overall approach with a view toward the multiple dimensions of audience perception.

As an audience member, then, put yourself in the role of a prospective investor listening to the presentations. At the end of the sales conference, each student may buy a total of fifty shares of stock divided among all presentations excluding one's own. In other words, one may invest heavily in a few presentations or invest less in a greater number. As an audience, you will need to devise a reliable means of notetaking so that investment decisions can be made at the end of the whole conference. As a speaker, this means you must plan a communication strategy both persuasive and memorable.

## SUMMARY

The end goal of business speech is to elicit a specific and favorable response from an audience in the form of actions taken or attitudes changed. Such response is based upon an audience member's assessment of the speech's merits. Our discussion in the previous chapter centered on descriptive aspects of audience perception; our attention in this chapter has turned to the evaluative dimension of audience response.

Consumers of business speech make three kinds of judgment, whether consciously or unconsciously. First, they assess speaker credibility. Before accepting as valid any speech proposition, one wants to know from whom the opinion comes: "Consider the source." Questions of credibility apply as much to evidence quoted in a speech as they do to the thought and performance of a speaker. Specifically, audiences determine speaker credibility by adding up four variables — prior reputation, knowledge, authority (including that conferred by association), and attitudes toward the topic and the listener.

A second category of judgment offered by audiences includes all assessments of the speech text — its content, language, style, and structure. Even if one were to read a speech transcript without having heard its delivery, myriad judgments could be made of the quality of information and its logical validity, *and* of an implied relationship between the speaker and the audience. Both parties are present in a text's language and organization as projections of attitude and expectations of response. Positive audience assessment of a speech text demands (1) language that reflects thorough preparation and complete analysis, (2) a pattern of organization that assists clear perception and that provides reliable recall, and (3) appeals for response that are reasonable and fair.

Too often audience assessment stops here. However, a third kind of judgment must be made to guarantee impartial evaluation. An audience member must test his or her own ability to respond fully and fairly to a particular speech. This self-criticism involves, first, determining whether one's prior knowledge of a subject qualifies one to judge the speech. Second, what vested interests might impede audience perception or distort their judgment? Third, is the audience member prepared fully to attend and to retain all communication dimensions of a speech event?

These three areas of audience assessment — speaker credibility, textual validity, and audience reliability — suggest judgment of, and response to, each component of a speech transaction. Establishing one's own standards of assessment and response is critical to speaker preparation and crucial to audience competence.

# 8

# The Text: Topic Selection and Research

Public speech demands an interplay among speaker, audience, and text. No one component alone can authorize or control the experience. Rather, there exists a network of minute links between the speaker's projected thought and perspective and the viewer's perceived meaning and response. These two individuals come together in a particular place for a particular occasion with a special purpose. Each has vested interests and personal (or corporate) prejudices. They become connected in space and over time. Helping to make those connections solid and reliable is a speech text—the content, diction, style, and structure of a public presentation. The text is, simply, language, but language is never simple. In this and the next two chapters, we look closely at how speech texts function in a business presentation. (Later, in Chapter 13, we shall consider the special circumstances of a speech text in print.)

## DIMENSIONS OF A SPEECH TEXT

In previous chapters, we examined two basic questions of business speech: who is speaking and to whom? Implicit in our answers were the related issues of "when" and "where." Now we must explore the "what" and the "how" of business speech, both aspects of language. Essentially, a text can be examined on four dimensions—information, diction, style, and structure.

*Information* is the "what" of speech, sometimes termed the content. A speaker has no more important decision to make than the choice of what information to include in a given speech and what to exclude. To leave out vital information or to offer inadequate support and explanation undermines communication. Similarly, to overload the audience with unnecessary data or trivial explanation reduces attention and deadens perception. No delivery, however polished, can make up for bad decisions at the level of a speech's information.

*Diction* refers to a text's specific vocabulary. Word choices are all-important to public communication. They represent an implied contract of meaning offered by the speaker and accepted or rejected by a listener. Words must be chosen for their communication efficiency and precision with regard to a given audience and a given topic. Individual words, if well chosen, can convey rich meaning and can be remembered long after the speech event. If poorly chosen (without thought or in haste), words will make apparent the bankruptcy of a speaker's thought, the inadequacy of his or her research, or a shallowness of commitment to a topic or an audience.

*Style*, another element of language, has to do particularly with a speaker's phrases, clauses, sentences, and paragraphs. Each person's distinctive style can be defined by characteristic ways that he or she combines words. Style has to do with syntax (word order) and sentence length. Style involves the rhythm or cadence of language. Even in print, style implies voice. That is, a silent reader hears the speaking voice in the inflection of a phrase and the pauses of punctuation.

A text's *structure* is its speaker's sequence of information—what comes first, second, and so on. Structure describes the distinctive shape of discourse. We shall see, in the succeeding two chapters, that efficient structures are designed to accommodate an audience's spatial and temporal perceptions.

Every speech text, good or bad, can be analyzed and evaluated on these four dimensions—information, diction, style, and structure. Our primary interest at present is in the first consideration, the *what* of business speech.

## TOPIC SELECTION

Topic selection may seem, at first thought, a mundane, apparently simple task. It isn't. The effective choice of a speech subject demands aptitude and skill. Right selection (correctly worded) can, of itself, predict success. A failure of communication may be anticipated when a speaker selects a topic without the necessary competence to address it, when an audience's interests and needs are not considered fully, or when a topic is unsuited to a given occasion. Each of these failures represents bad judgment—a faulty analysis of self, others, or context. Of course, some speakers avoid altogether the proper selection of a topic and, thereby, abandon all conscious control of the communicative act. A speech topic, selected carefully and worded precisely, is like the thesis statement of an essay. It identifies a *subject*, defines its *scope*, and reveals the speaker's *perspective*. Implicit in this combination is an expectation of *response* from the audience.

A public speaker who lacks experience often confuses topic selection with the identification of some broad subject area. He or she decides to give a talk about "employee morale" or "corporate profits" or "government regulation." These headings may serve as starting points for a speaker's thought, but they do not impel one toward composition. The ultimate selection and statement of a topic should suggest a meaningful shape for the speech event. For instance, the above subjects could become manageable speech topics if given scope and perspective, as follows:

"I'd like to address the declining [perspective] employee morale [subject] in the research department [limitation of place] over the past few months [limitation of time]."

Or

"I shall chart the optimal range [perspective] of corporate profits [subject] over the next two quarters [limitation]."

Or

"I propose a reasoned reduction [perspective] of federal regulation [subject] of the banking industry [limitation]."

These statements leave still unanswered many questions about the development of their respective speeches, but each provides a solid foundation for beginning work.

An effective text must be based upon the speaker's deliberate grasp of a subject, its scope, and his or her own perspective. The actual statement of a topic may or may not appear verbatim in a speech's language. There are myriad ways of revealing topic selection without announcing a thesis. However, a speaker's preparation must begin with a clear statement, and audience perception should end with a firm grasp of that intention.

## RESEARCH

A well-defined speech topic points the speaker in useful directions for research. This important stage of preparation entails the collection of quantitative (predictive) and qualitative (descriptive) data. It demands reading, accurate note taking, and a system for categorizing evidence. The results of a speaker's research, good or bad, will be evident on several dimensions of speech text. The quality of one's research is manifest in the speaker's sense of authority, in the text's logical validity, and in its persuasive appeal to an audience.

Research is best conducted in response to a specific question. For example, "Why has productivity declined over the past six months?" Or, "How can we change the public perception of our product line to reach older consumers, as well as young people?" Any fair and full answer to a research question demands valid evidence and compels the researcher to make a careful investigation.

Methods of research vary widely—from scientific inquiry to historical scholarship to polls, surveys, and interviews. Whatever the means of data collection, and regardless of the results, the function of research in speech preparation remains the same: to provide a foundation in fact and interpretation upon which a speaker's argument and appeal may be based. To the audience, research serves in a support role. That is, the results of research are usually summarized briefly and appear as subpoints in a text's outline. To the speaker, however, research is primary. From its thoroughness and logical validity emerge the main points of discourse.

Research should shape every dimension of a speech text. Systematic inquiry into any subject can generate useful *information*, provide precise *diction*, dictate an appropriate *style*, and suggest a helpful *structure*. In one text, a speaker's research is apparent by specific references to methodology or outside resources. In another, research serves simply as the background for a speaker's authority.

When investigating any general business topic, the speaker has nearly limitless resources in a good library. Three useful starting points are the *Business Periodical Index* (BPI), *The Wall Street Journal Index*, and *The New York Times Index*. Remember, when quoting authorities or referring to any outside resource, the same principles of documentation and plagiarism apply to speech as to composition. You *must* cite all references to another person's research or language. Copyright law restricts the reproduction of published material in both print and speech.

## COMPOSITION

Correct topic selection and thorough research are absolutes of the speech process, without which reliable communication is impossible. By this point in speech preparation, one has determined a subject, defined its limits, articulated one's own point of view, and done the necessary homework to address that subject with authority. Composition, the next step, may be defined generally as a process giving discernible shape to discourse. Speech composition, thus, is akin to written composition. It is álso related to musical composition, to page make-up in journalism, to arrangement in photography or painting, even to team membership in athletics or business. Speech composition gives meaningful shape to communication with an audience because it links a speaker's intention with a listener's perceptions. Composition is related to delivery, but they are not the same thing. Composition is a predelivery process. During this phase of speech preparation, ideas and languages are still malleable; whereas, delivery gives a fixed form to communication.

There are three basic approaches to speech composition. These are not mutually exclusive, but each describes a distinct viewpoint toward the speech act and, thus, each merits individual attention. The first approach is based upon a traditional *outline* with main points and subpoints connected by a straight line of logic. This visual or spatial model of speech communication has an obvious advantage. By an outline's rigor and efficiency, every sentence is guaranteed to contribute to an overall structure. The visual appeal of an outline is, also, its greatest weakness. Audience perception, as we have observed, is not simply or solely spatial. It occurs over time, and the astute speaker must take into account this temporal variable when designing a strategy for communication.

The second approach to composition is based upon a *flow chart*. This modified outline acknowledges the effect of time upon audience perception by its horizontal rather than vertical orientation and by its very name (i.e., "flow" or "fluid" chart). A flow chart is a time line of discourse set up not to describe a speaker's intention (as does the vertical outline) but to predict and control audience perception. The best way to design a flow chart for speech is to start with its two end points—a description of audience knowledge and perspective at the beginning of a speech, which is indicated on the left end, and a prediction of changes in knowledge and viewpoint by the end of the speech, which is noted on the right. The following illustration is an example of a flow chart.

where the audience begins
(i.e., prior knowledge,
attitude, and viewpoint)

where the audience should end
(i.e., new information, changed
attitude, and altered viewpoint)

Along this time line, then, one marks the turning points in audience perception that are required to affect a desired change. The similarities between an outline and a flow chart are obvious, but the distinctions remain great. One is spatial and speaker-oriented; the other temporal and audience-oriented. One is vertical and rigid; the other horizontal and fluid. Because a flow chart describes the speech event from a listener's viewpoint, the speaker is more likely, when using the approach, to bear in mind an audience's needs and interests. Furthermore, once a person has become accustomed to the flow chart method of preparation, its image should serve as a useful aid in speech delivery.

These first two approaches to composition, outlining and flow charting, require pen and paper to link verbal and written communication. A third approach, both the newest and the oldest model, is *oral composition*. This is an approach that defines the speech act as a verbal activity from beginning to end. Oral composition is *not* off-the-cuff delivery but an experience of disciplined rehearsal, of actual speech practice from experimentation through revision to polish. Oral composition moves the speech act away from its typical relationship to writing toward a traditional relationship with storytelling. Oral composition underscores the essentially narrative nature of speech. It is related to the flow chart by an interest in time and perception, but this approach insists upon orality as the primary shaping experience of speech preparation. Until one has tried oral composition, revising a speech time and again through rehearsal, the approach may seem foreign and unproductive. However, with discipline and attention, the approach will prove both fruitful and economical.

One rule of thumb when attempting oral composition is to invest an hour of rehearsal for each minute of actual speech delivery. While this may seem an extraordinary time investment, it is equivalent to the ratio of hours to pages in written composition. Remember that this kind of rehearsal-composition can go on in free minutes any time during the day. One need not (indeed, should not) set aside hours of continuous work. The process operates best in a succession of short rehearsal periods. A second rule of thumb is to practice oral composition while standing or walking, never while sitting. Human speech and motion are linked integrally to one another. The act of walking helps to ensure a sensible rhythm in speech patterns just as walking helps the actor to memorize lines or the conductor to learn a musical score.

The individual in business who makes public speeches frequently will, no doubt, evolve his or her own approach to preparation. The three approaches suggested here (i.e., the outline, the flow chart, and oral composition) reflect slightly different viewpoints or orientations toward the speech activity. However, the sequence of major stages in text preparation remains unalterable—topic selection, research, composition. Each phase is linked naturally to the other two, but their order cannot be reversed without doing real damage to the prospects of effective communication.

## EXERCISES

**A**   Read this transcript and answer the questions that follow regarding dimensions of the speech's text. This speech was delivered by Barzun Bate, president of Food Services Corporation, a contract management firm that operates institutional food services (e.g., for schools, hospitals, and industries). The speech was delivered at the company's annual meeting of shareholders and represents a presidential report of corporate growth and progress over the previous year. The speech came early on in the program, after the welcome and chairman's report and before a period of question and answers and the announcement of election results for new corporate officers. To deliver this speech, Mr. Bate stood at a lectern and read verbatim from a typed manuscript. The audience numbered approximately 360.

I trust that you have had an opportunity to look over our annual report and its statistics of corporate revenue and profits. I'd like to take a few minutes now to underline the more salient statistics as they relate to corporate operations—my bailiwick.

1982 was a banner year of growth for FSC with an 18 percent increase in operating revenues, a 23 percent increase in net income, a 20 percent increase in earnings per share, and a 22 percent increase in cash dividends. Our total assets increased by 23 percent during the year, and we utilized these effectively in establishing an asset-to-revenue turnover of approximately sevenfold. Our incremental return in investment increased from 56.07 percent to 62.3 percent and we were able to pay out 59 percent of our net earnings in dividends. We also improved our rate of return on average shareholders' equity to 35.7 percent from 33.2 percent, and we improved our cash and cash equivalent position by 28 percent.

This is the kind of performance you have come to expect from Food Services Corporation, and we're proud to meet those expectations even in the current state of recession affecting the service industries nationwide. In addition to constant growth in our staple services, we have expanded services by implementing the first action steps of our targeted long-range planning plan. We are moving into the educational market with significant numbers, adding 57 new college, university, or community college facilities to the account list begun in 1981. This growth represents a 56 percent increase. In the health care field, we have added 142 new hospitals and over 100 special care and nursing facilities. Our share of the health care market has increased from 42 percent to 48 percent, a remarkable jump in one year.

With our diversification of interests to additional institutions, we have evolved new operational strategies. We are decentralizing operations whenever possible, moving operational units close to the customer, and making each one accountable on a profit center basis. In the past year alone, we instituted 36 new subdivisions within our 8 geographical regions. This reorganization has demanded the addition of three new vice-presidential posts ably filled by George Martin, Browning Kirby, and Phyllis D'Angelo.

These changes in markets and operations promise continued profit growth in the future for Food Service Corporation. We have reason for confidence in the future and appreciate your continuing share in the enterprises of FSC, your investment in an industry responsive to market needs and opportunities.

1. In a well-developed paragraph, analyze the *information* level of this text. Characterize the kinds of information included, and make note of any important exclusions. Evaluate the communication effectiveness of this presentation of information.

2. In one paragraph, describe and evaluate the speaker's *diction*. What do his word choices indicate about the speaker's knowledge, attitude, and viewpoints toward his subject and his audience?

3. Read this brief transcript aloud, and analyze its oral *style*. What are the merits and demerits of this speaker's rhythm and voice?

4. Describe and evaluate the text's *structure*, its sequence of parts. To make such an analysis, you must take into account the speaker's apparent purpose and probable audience.

**B**   Practice the skills required for effective topic selection. Within each subject area listed below, design a specific topic suited to a ten-minute speech for which the speaker would be given two weeks for preparation. Write a one-sentence description of each topic selected, following the models on page 108. Be sure that your statement includes clear definitions of subject, scope, and perspective.

1. American labor

2. Employee profit-sharing

3. Corporate public relations

4. Product safety

5. Foreign competition

6. Multinational corporations

7. Dow Jones average

8. Local ownership

9. Small businesses

10. Federal money supply

**C**   For each topic in exercise B, design a research approach for the preparation of a speech text. That is, if you were given two weeks to prepare a ten-minute speech on each topic that you selected, how would you conduct the necessary research? Be specific in terms of the experiments you might design and the resources or references you might consult in the research.

1. American labor

2. Employee profit-sharing

3. Corporate public relations

4. Product safety

5. Foreign competition

6. Multinational corporations

7. Dow Jones average

8. Local ownership

9. Small businesses

10. Federal money supply

**D**   Now select three of your speech topics from exercises B and C, and practice the approaches to composition discussed in this chapter.

1. For the first topic, create an outline. Develop each main point (Roman numeral) with logical subpoints (upper-case letters) and specific evidence (Arabic numerals).

2. For the second topic, create a horizontal flow chart. Identify specifically the probable starting point for audience perception and the desired end point. Note at least four specific turning points of perception between the text's beginning and ending.

3. For the third topic, try out the approach of oral composition during a one-week rehearsal period. For each of seven days, allow yourself two 20-minute rehearsals, one in the morning and one in the evening. Keep a journal noting specifically what you did at each rehearsal, the changes made, and your evaluation of the evolving speech.

## SAMPLE SPEECH

The following manuscript was written by Dr. Mary Lou Higgerson for a speech that she gave on February 19, 1979 to over one hundred insurance executives. Entitled "The First Encounter," the text addresses the importance of initiating interpersonal relationships, particularly those in business, with good communication behavior. Dr. Higgerson speaks frequently to business groups on subjects related to organizational communication. She has evolved a method of preparation combining outlining with a modified oral composition. She selects a topic, does the required research, and spends considerable time developing an outline. After this thorough preparation, then, she writes quickly at the typewriter, and she projects into the language, style, and structure her own speaking voice and a clear awareness of the audience.

---

### THE FIRST ENCOUNTER

Has it occurred to you that you are about to hear some information regarding first encounters from a person that you are encountering for the first time? Does that make you a little nervous? Well I can tell you it makes me a little nervous, because I know how important first encounters can be in determining any future encounters we might have.

Most of what we accomplish in life — both professionally and personally — hinges on our ability to relate with other people. Furthermore, problems we face are usually the result of our failure to relate effectively to other people. For example, have you ever noticed how the same message can get two different reactions? Think of some of the ways in which you have approached clients and their responses to what you said. Have you ever said something like, "I understand from your friend, Tom Smith, that you need some help in planning your estate." The reaction you secure to that statement could range from "I sure do, pleased to meet you." — to "What does he mean, I need help?" The perfectly right thing to say at one moment to one client can be the perfectly wrong thing to say at another moment to a different client.

We are caught in a double bind because man is a social being and he needs people. We have to be able to relate to people. We have to make others understand what we want, what we are trying to say, and at the same time we have to understand their needs in order to adapt our ideas and communicate them in such a way that they do solicit the desired response. In short, we need to learn how to "handle" people and that requires an ability to perceive people.

Our need to be able to relate to others is so important that we begin cultivating our interpersonal skills at perceiving people when we are young children. It doesn't take a child very long to learn that he can perform differently at his grandparent's house than he can at home. Similarly, at a very early age, an infant will learn to distinguish his father from other men. He learns to treat his dad differently than he treats strange men. And usually, embarrassed mothers are very grateful when the child learns this distinction.

Sociologists such as George Herbert Mead and Hugh Duncan have labeled this process "learning to play the game." These theorists argue there are two subidentities within each individual. One is termed the "I" and that is the portion of an individual that reflects his own attributes, beliefs, and ideas. The other subidentity is termed the "me." The "me" represents a collection of opinions that an individual carries around in his head about how other people would react to what he says, does, or believes. The theory is that before an individual articulates an idea, he imagines in his own mind what the response will be. For example, one man might say to himself "When my spouse learns that I'll be late for dinner again tonight, she will. . . . " We learn to anticipate the reaction of others to what we say, do, or think. Just as a child soon learns which behavior is rewarded and which behavior is punished.

While children learn at a very early age how to "play the game" of perceiving other people, as adults we need to be masters of it. We need to know how to approach a prospective client. And yes. . . we need to know how to explain to our spouses that we won't be home for dinner for the fifth night in a row. If we look at each of these examples more closely, it will help us discover how we learn to "play the game" or "read people." Think what you do when you are trying to determine how to approach a prospective client. Don't you start by making some assessment of what type of person that client is? You may have been through some sales training programs which taught you how to categorize people into subgroups of personality types. When you go through this process you are doing what Mead and Duncan have called "playing the game" or what people in communication term perceiving people. More simply, you are trying to understand the other person in order to relate more effectively.

Take the second example that I mentioned, where you need to know how to explain to your spouse that you won't be home for dinner for the fifth night in a row. This situation is not a first encounter, but you are still in the business of needing to read people. I'd like to use this example to make an important point. It's very possible to have a first encounter with a person that you have known for quite some time, if the situation makes it a new encounter. Such situations are easily detected when you find yourself saying "John never acted like that before," or "I couldn't believe that was Joan." So whether you are meeting someone for the first time or experiencing a first encounter with someone you have known previously, your success at relating to other people hinges on your ability to accurately perceive and adapt to that person.

First encounters are important to us. In fact we typically give more thought and worry to a first encounter than we do to meeting with a long-time acquaintance.

(First), we become more conscious of our dress in a first encounter. "What should I wear?" "Will wearing a vest make me look too formal?" "Can I get by without a tie?" Are these familiar questions that you have asked yourself upon occasion? And if you remember the occasion when you found yourself asking such questions, chances are it was not when you were about to meet an old acquaintance. Rather, it was when you were about to have a first encounter.

(Second), we plan what we will say. Before meeting a prospective client for the first time, you might say to yourself, "I'll start by asking about his family," or "I know he's a Shriner, so I'll ask about that last campaign they had to raise funds for the Children's Hospital." Have you ever made a conscious decision before meeting someone as to what topics you would talk about? But that's not all you do before a first encounter.

(Third), we actually plan our attitude. Remember those pep talks you give yourself as you drive or as you walk through the door to a meeting. With confidence "I'm going to sell $50,000 worth of life." You are planning your attitude.

(Fourth), we are concerned about the image we make in first encounters. In fact, so concerned, that we rehearse dialogues in our mind. We anticipate what the other person will say. Before a sales presentation, you might rehearse the following: "He'll probably ask me why an individual plan is better than a group plan and I'll tell him. . . ." Have you done these things? Sure. We all have. Do we spend that much time on an old acquaintance? No. Unless the situation makes an old acquaintance a first encounter. And you may find yourself in a first encounter with an old acquaintance when you are about to make a sales presentation to a friend with whom you have only played tennis.

We work very hard at having successful first encounters. We work hard to make the right impression. I've already mentioned how we concentrate on our dress, the conversation, our attitude and our image. But have you ever wondered how we know what is proper dress, the right conversation, or the appropriate attitude? How do we know what makes a favorable impression on other people? Think about it for a moment. Is there any logic to why men tend to wear a three-piece business suit to important meetings? Is the three-piece business suit really that comfortable? As comfortable as that favorite pair of old jeans you wear on Saturday? And yet, vests are worn more often in situations in which comfort would be an asset.

We also have definite concepts of what is a good image. We work hard to project an image that indicates such positive traits as mature, responsible, serious, or businesslike. But have you ever stopped to wonder what makes those positive traits? Why aren't we impressed with the nonserious person? Their blood pressure is probably a lot better than that of a serious person. Still, we have definite concepts of what is appropriate dress, the right conversation, and a favorable image.

We acquire these definite concepts from society. We live in a society dominated by mass communication and, consequently, the media influence our lives. T.V. commercials, the characters portrayed on television programs, the books that we read, the songs that we hear on the radio, the articles which appear in the magazines we read. . . . These are just a few examples of the significant impact media have in shaping what we see as appropriate. From these things we get role models. We can learn what it is like to be a teacher by watching "Kotter," to be a prosperous businessperson by watching "Dallas," to be a father of eight by watching "Eight is Enough," or to be a lawyer by watching "Kaz." We seem to have a program for any possible occupation. From such T.V. programs and movies we form stereotypes about different occupational roles and different personality types.

The media also dictate what personality traits and attitudes are desirable. One popular advertising strategy makes use of ideal images in such a way that the consumer is made to feel second-rate until he/she buys the product. Think of the commercials you have heard—I mean...  "Do you care enough to send the very best?" and please remember that all "Choosy mothers choose Jiff" and most importantly "Does your family have a piece of the rock?" or "Are you the type of person who worries about not being in the picture?"

We not only learn that it is important to please others, but we learn *how* to please others. After all, it's . . . "Stuffing instead of potatoes anytime." And isn't it comforting to know that the cake was so good that he "Couldn't wait 'till it was frosted." And what a relief to realize that "He noticed" that the fabric softener had been added to the wash. And we must remember that "Gentlemen prefer Hanes." And "All her men wear English Leather or they wear nothing at all." T.V. commercials are just one way in which we are influenced. Listen to the song titles that you hear. "You Are the Sunshine of My Life," "I Can't Make It Without You," "All I ever Need Is You." What about food, clothing, and shelter? While the theme expressed in these song titles is not realistic or practical, we don't question it. In fact, don't we look for, expect, and cherish that attitude in a spouse? If you are still unconvinced of the impact media have on our attitudes and behavior, simply notice some of the books being published. We have a book for every aspect of human life. We have books entitled, *Body Language*, *After the First Four Seconds*, *What Do You Say After Hello?* or *Winning with People*. How many of you have read these or similar books? I'm not surprised. That is an indication that you work at having successful first encounters. For that, you deserve to be complimented. In communication, we refer to these books as the self-help...or how-to books. . . . They typically make good reading because they are packed full of examples with which the reader can identify. The shortcoming of these books is that they leave the reader with an awareness of the need for more effective communication, but without any improvement in communication skill. There is a significant difference between knowing something is important to do and being able to do it. In my work, we start with an awareness of the need for effective communication, but focus on improving skills which result in more effective communication.

I will discuss this in more detail later. For now, simply remember the reason I reviewed some of the current T.V. commercials, song titles, and book titles with you...that is, that the media have a strong impact in determining what we perceive as appropriate attitudes and behavior. Armed with the information we receive from the media, we work hard at making a "good" impression in our first encounters.

But that's not all we do to have a successful first encounter. We use references whenever possible. These are the people who recommend us to that new person. Haven't you often asked a client, "Can I tell Mr. Newberry that you sent me?" Or how about the letter of introduction that is fairly common in business? You know the letter that begins "Recently our office has had the pleasure of serving your friend, Mr. Goodneighbor, and he indicated to us that you might be in need of our services." This is a common business practice, which is done to make a first encounter go a bit smoother.

We also collect data on the person we are about to meet. We're appreciative of any label we might get from other people who know that person. To find out that a prospective client is a "Mason" or "civic-minded" can be very informative. We collect biographic data such as age, education level, place of work, position held, or length of employment. Some salespeople keep notecards on prospective clients.

We also look for elements that we have in common with a new person. Similarities in background such as "We both grew up near Springfield," or "We both work in sales" can provide a basis for establishing a good rapport with a prospective client. Consequently, we devote time and energy to finding areas of common ground. We even do this when meeting a stranger without advance notice. On my last trip to New York, I met an attorney while waiting for my return flight. The weather was bad, most of the planes were late, and conversations with other stranded passengers helped to pass the time. As most conversations begin, we talked about the weather and our resulting predicament with slow airplanes. Once these topics had been exhausted, we started talking about geographics. I was asked where I live and when I explained that I was from Illinois, his immediate response was "Illinois! I knew someone from Illinois once. Do you know Al Pioneer?" Now, common sense should tell us that it's very unlikely, given the size and population of Illinois, that I would know Al Pioneer. And yet, we don't find it strange at all when we are asked such questions by new acquaintances. We will simply take any opportunity to find an element of common ground. In fact, my own response in that situation was "No. I don't know Al Pioneer, but I do know Larry Grypp and Paul Piche."

So far, I have talked about those things we do prior to the actual encounter, such as determining our dress, thinking about what image we want to project, using references, collecting data, and trying to find elements of common ground. Although these are important steps, probably our largest input for perceiving people comes from the impressions we get of that person in the actual encounter. Right now you are forming a perception of me and I'm forming one of you.

We perceive character traits. We use physical features such as a smile, eyes, or posture to tell us about emotional states. Whether a person is happy, sad, overworked, hungover, or any number of things. We use our own past experiences in dealing with other people to form perceptions of new people we meet. For example—you might discover and say to yourself "The last time a prospective client said they didn't need additional insurance, I sold a big policy. Therefore, I know not to give up when a prospective client tells me he doesn't need additional insurance." We are more prone to form perceptions of emotional states than physical characteristics. We can meet and chat with someone for the first time and walk away with an impression. But chances are we don't walk away with the impression that he was a tall, slender fellow. While we might certainly be aware of that, we are much more likely to walk away with an impression such as he is an ambitious individual. We're much more prone to form perceptions of a person's personality than we are to make mental notes of his physical traits. Think about the adjectives that you use to describe other people. Do you find yourself saying, "He is a tall, blue-eyed person"? No. You are more likely to say, "He's a friendly person."

Perhaps this is why we spend so much time thinking about the image we project in a first encounter. Remember earlier I mentioned that it is typical for us to plan what attitude we want to portray. We say to ourselves that we are going to be confident, or caring. This is not easy. There has been a lot of research done by people in communication on credibility. Basically, the research tells us that a person with high credibility is perceived as having three character traits: competence, trustworthiness, and good will toward other people. Sounds logical, right? The research on credibility also tells us that a person who is perceived as credible is much more successful in persuading other people. Obviously, it is desirable for a person in sales to be perceived as credible. I've just told you that one aspect of being perceived as credible is demonstrating competence. But how does one "look" competent? Let's try it. Would you all please adopt a competent look. Oh, that was your competent look? How does a person look competent? I'm teasing with you, but it helps me make a point. Remember, I mentioned earlier that there is a difference between knowing something is important to do and how to do it. This is my criticism of those "self-help" or "how-to" books. It is not enough to tell people in sales that you need to appear competent. In fact, I argue that most people in sales already know that. What they may not know is *how* to increase their chances of being perceived as competent. That is a *skill* which can be taught and developed in training programs, but which can only be discussed in books and speeches.

It's not easy to project a particular trait. Yet, at the same time it is impossible to remain void of expression. Have you ever tried to look neutral? Would you turn to the person seated next to you and look neutral. Neighbors, is that a neutral look? Or is it a look of apathy, boredom, or frustration? At times, you may intend to remain neutral, but it is not uncommon to have someone else perceive an expression that is not neutral. Probably the best example of this is the old argument over what is wrong when actually nothing is wrong. When the first person says to the second person "What's wrong?" and the second person responds "Nothing." The first person replies, "There is something wrong, now what's wrong?" And the second person, becoming a bit more irritated, repeats "Nothing's wrong." And the first thing you know, something is wrong. It's not easy to project the image we chose. Yet, some image will be projected because the person at the other end is always forming a perception.

No matter what perception we form, whether we're right or wrong, we relate to people and we respond to people on the basis of our perception of them. Isn't it true that a good sales technique is to obtain input about the prospective client and then adjust the sales presentation to that client's particular personality? And isn't it true that often your success at making a sale to a prospective client hinges on how accurately you perceive that person's needs and how well you adapted your sales presentation?

Consequently, we need to do more than work hard at first encounters. We must be successful at them. And as I have indicated, our success in first encounters hinges upon our skill in accurately perceiving people, as well as accurately relating to what we perceive. Unfortunately, accurate perceptions of people are not easy to obtain. It is possible to have two people with the same background information on a prospective client meet that client at the same time and still have them reach two different conclusions about the client and about what approach should be used in the sales presentation. This probably happens when a new agent is being trained by calling on prospective clients with an experienced agent present.

Similarly, two people can form different perceptions of us in a single situation. Right now, if I were to ask each of you to list adjectives that describe me, I doubt that you would all agree. We each have a slightly different set of past experiences and we have different preferences for interpreting the information we obtain about a person. For example, I have a strong respect for competence. I admire people who are good at what they do. So when I perceive a person as competent, I am much more tolerant of other personality traits which may irritate other people. I will tolerate a certain amount of curtness in a competent person. Some of you may have a preference for politeness. If so, you would perceive the competent, but curt, individual less favorably than I would. Similarly, some people respect the professional who puts family ahead of work and other people respect the professional who puts work ahead of family.

Because it is possible to have two people form different perceptions of the same person, it is difficult to be certain that our perceptions are accurate. This is especially true because our perceptions are based on more than the other person we are perceiving. We perceive people from a framework of our own past experiences and through a framework of how we perceive ourself. Did you ever have a bad day when you just didn't feel very good about yourself? It definitely colors the perceptions you form about other people you may meet. The situation can also affect the perceptions we form. Meeting a person for the first time at a party will prompt a different perception than meeting that same person for the first time in a professional situation. Finally, our perceptions of other people are affected by our sense abilities. Any limitations we have with regard to sight or hearing will affect the perceptions we form.

It may seem as though I have painted a very grim picture. I have confirmed that encounters are important to us and that we work hard at making them successful. However, I have also demonstrated that successful first encounters only take place when we form accurate perceptions of other people. Unfortunately, accurate perceptions are difficult to obtain. Although the task is difficult, the situation is not hopeless. Even though it is true that individual differences make it impossible to outline specific rules for deriving a particular perception of a peculiar or particular situation, there are certain skills which can be learned to help you become more proficient in perceiving other people. Frankly, this is why I prefer to conduct workshops which are directed at improving perception skills than to give speeches on the importance of perception skills. In a workshop for fifteen or fewer people, I can focus on developing and improving those perception skills which help each participant become more effective in relating to other people. Unfortunately, the most assistance I can offer a group this size is to provide some guiding principles which can be helpful in forming any perception.

1. *Be aware of your perceptual framework for perceiving others.* Stand back and try to become a third-person observer about how you personally form perceptions of other people. What are your preferences? Do you prefer people who put family ahead of work, or people who put work ahead of family? Or do you trust well-groomed people more than others? Learn to recognize your preferences. This insight will help you detect inaccurate perceptions.

2. *Consider the source* of any information you receive about a person. Is the source reliable? Is your source in a position to know what he is telling you? Date the information. If you are told that Sam Bunker is crazy because he told jokes across Europe in WWII, please remember that Sam may be different today.
3. *Be sensitive to the situation.* Maybe Ed denied being interested in additional health insurance because you asked him in front of his employer. Above all, try to read the interaction from the other person's perspective.
4. *Be flexible.* Be willing to update your perceptions of other people. If you find it difficult to say "I was wrong," perhaps you can say "I didn't have the total picture."

## DISCUSSION QUESTIONS

1. A rhetorical question is one that implies its own answer or that suggests an obvious answer. This speaker uses many rhetorical questions. Find instances of this strategy in the manuscript and evaluate their communication effectiveness. Does each rhetorical question serve the same function?
2. This manuscript takes 30-40 minutes in delivery—a long speech. Discuss the structural devices used to aid audience perception. That is, describe how the speaker moves from point to point, how she makes major transitions, and how she summarizes progress through the text.
3. At two points, this speaker asks her audience to appear "competent" and "neutral." Discuss the communication advantages and disadvantages of this strategy of audience participation.
4. This speech is about first encounters and itself represents a first encounter. From the manuscript alone, profile the speaker—her knowledge, authority, and viewpoints toward the subject and the audience. Develop your arguments with specific evidence from the text.
5. Evaluate the communication merits and demerits of this speech text.

## HYPOTHETICAL SPEECH

Imagine that you are the director of personnel for a large company. At an orientation session for new employees, your staff must explain all available options for insurance coverage. In a 4-5 minute speech, explain the major kinds of life insurance available today. With an increasing diversity of life insurance plans, you will need to do research to ensure adequate coverage of the subject. The purpose of this speech is not to persuade the audience to adopt one policy over another but to *describe* the defining differences among life insurance options. Assume that your audience knows little about the subject and, thus, take care to define all technical terms.

## SUMMARY

The effectiveness of a speech text can be measured by four variables — its information, diction, style, and structure. Information refers to a speech's content. Proper analysis of this dimension centers on the appropriateness of a speaker's choices of what information to include and what to exclude. Diction refers to another kind of choice that a speaker must make — vocabulary. Individual word choices can say a great deal about a speaker's knowledge, authority, and point of view. Words, if well chosen, also can serve as the contract for shared meaning between a speaker and the audience. Style is a broad term used to describe the distinctive patterns of an individual's speech. At a basic level, the consideration of style must include sentence length, sentence construction, and syntax. Style has to do especially with the rhythm of speech — both its thought and delivery. Structure, then, is the largest feature of a text's profile. It entails sequence and transition; it describes the overall shape of a given speech.

The creation of an effective speech text must begin with proper topic selection. A well-worded topic, like the thesis statement of an essay, identifies a subject, defines its scope, and reveals the speaker's perspective.

Precise topic selection leads one naturally toward useful research — the collection and interpretation of quantitative and qualitative data. Competent research, whether its results appear in the foreground or the background of a text, underscores the speaker's authority to address a given issue. Research is conducted most efficiently in response to a specific question or a set of questions central to the speech topic.

After topic selection and research, one is ready for composition — the conscious process of giving discernible shape to discourse. Three approaches to this phase of speech preparation are the outline, the flow chart, and oral composition.

# 9

# The Text: Information and Language

Every business speech tells something for a purpose. Its text must transmit information and affect persuasion. Each decision of composition or delivery that a speaker makes should enhance the informative impact or persuasive appeal of the speech as a whole. In this chapter and the next, we shall look closely at these two aspects of a speech text. The present focus is on information exchange, particularly on the relationship between information and language. Chapter 10, then, will direct attention to rhetorical strategies, especially the links between persuasion and structure.

In speech communication, *all* information is tied up with language. Even numbers are spoken as words. Even nonverbal cues are perceived in relation to verbal discourse. Even tone of voice is made manifest by the inflection of language. The information presented in a speech is bound up altogether in words, and any speaker determined to achieve communication, to get a point across, must take language seriously.

## INTENTION AND PERCEPTION

At no level of a speech text is the difference between a speaker's intention and a listener's perception more apparent than in the language used. We have returned time and again to this theme of tension between a speaker's and a listener's viewpoints, so important is it to a practical understanding of the communication process. We are accustomed in everyday conversation to treating language lightly as the common and mundane possession of all adult users, and we neglect thus to respect its complexity and volatility. A public speaker makes this same mistake at great peril to a speech's potential. Words *are* the common possession of a speaker and an audience, but they possess uncommon qualities. Words are not static containers of meaning, but dynamic conveyors of intention and perception, voice and viewpoint, culture and personality. At the least, one must always look at the effect of a given word from two viewpoints—the speaker's and the listener's. Until a word comes to mean the same thing to both individuals, communication is impossible, and miscommunication is likely. In the case of a public speaking situation with many listeners present, the problem of achieving shared meaning for any given word becomes even more complicated than in one-to-one conversation. In business, sales are made or not made, policies are followed or ignored, viewpoints are clarified or confused, employee morale is enhanced or diminished all on the basis of a speaker's language usage.

We observed in earlier discussions of the speaker that language serves business best when it is straighforward, concise, and forceful. A careful speaker relies on the denotative, rather than the connotative, meanings of words. He or she selects the simplest term available for conveying a given idea and avoids unnecessary jargon. These stylistic virtues, if achieved, help to ensure common understanding between speaker and audience. The underlying mandate of a business speaker's word selection is to choose terms that say exactly what one wants to say *and* that are likely to be understood and remembered by an audience: choose words to guarantee the union of intention and perception.

Effective language usage demands of a speaker a rich and varied vocabulary from which to choose and the capacity to anticipate an audience's knowledge, interests, and needs. All our discussions of speech to this point have been based upon the fact that communication depends equally upon *what* is said and *who* says it. This linkage of speech and speaker in the perceptions of an audience occurs at the level of a text's language. Words express both a subject and a viewpoint; they convey a topic while reflecting their speaker's attitudes, prejudices, and feelings. The dual goals of business communication are to find language that presents information fully and that projects its speaker accurately. To achieve either goal without the other is to undermine credibility, to confuse the audience, or (in the worst case) to perpetrate a fraud.

One of the most interesting examples of a public speech that manipulated these variables of intention and perception was the now classic campaign rhetoric of George Smathers in his bid to unseat incumbent Senator Claude Pepper. Smathers used language with the apparent objective of putting down his opponent in the eyes of voters. Notice that there is nothing libelous in the language itself. The speaker's intention of casting Pepper in a bad light relied totally on an assumption of the audience's ignorance of certain words:

> Are you aware that Claude Pepper is known all over Washington as a shameless extrovert? Not only that, but this man is reliably reported to practice nepotism with his sister-in-law, and he has a sister who was once a thespian in wicked New York. Worst of all it is an established fact that Mr. Pepper before his marriage habitually practiced celibacy.

Furthermore, Claude Pepper had the audacity to matriculate at our home state university in full view of a major portion of the student body.[1]

The technique represented in this speech text is not recommended—except, perhaps, for comic effect. Whereas playing upon the misperceptions of an audience may, on occasion, yield short-term gains, it is guaranteed over time to ruin a speaker's reputation. (Observe that Claude Pepper, supposed victim of Smathers' rhetorical ruse, went on to more than thirty additional years of distinguished service in Congress.) In business speech, the penalties for ineffective language usage are both personal and corporate.

## KINDS OF WORDS

For organizing information and presenting it with impact, a speaker may draw upon three kinds of words. Each is appropriate to business communication, and the combination of all three allows the speaker to address a wide range of issues and audiences. These types of words represent types of thinking; one speaker will not be equally comfortable in using all three. Nevertheless, an individual who seeks to reach the greatest number of constituencies on the greatest array of topics must study all three uses of language.

The first kind of word is *declarative*. This category includes all terms that represent directly ideas or propositions. Declaration is the language of logical argument. *Imagery* is the second kind of word, and its appeal is to the senses. Word-images evoke mental pictures, smells, tastes, sounds, and tactile, thermal, or kinesthetic sensations. The human brain processes images and ideas differently; yet, both can be conveyed and evoked by language. The third kind of word is *figurative*—the expression of an idea or sensation through indirection. Under this heading are included such rhetorical and poetic devices as metaphor, simile, and personification.

Each type of word offers profound potentialities to the business speaker. These categories, on the one hand, describe language too simply and, on the other, offer general distinctions that can prove useful to a beginning speaker. Declarative language appeals primarily to the intellect, imagery to the senses, and figurative language to the imagination. Actually, one's imagination, senses, intellect, and emotions form a closely bound community of selves. Decisions are made and actions taken in response to these internal perspectives, a committee in miniature. A good speaker, intent upon full and memorable communication with an audience, must learn to *think* propositionally, imagistically, and figuratively and then to *speak* in language appropriate to each viewpoint.

[1] "Florida—Anything Goes," *Time*, 55 (April 17, 1950), p.38.

## LEVELS OF LANGUAGE

Until now, we have viewed information as conveyed by individual words. In addition, speech texts may be analyzed by the typical level of language used. Verbal expression may be categorized by four levels of language usage — formal, informal, casual, and intimate. The *formal* level is typified by a lecture, inaugural address, or other high pronouncement. Formal speech uses the general pronoun (one), shows little interest in establishing a relationship between speaker and audience, and rarely (if ever) uses humor. In business, formal speech may be appropriate for certain press releases and corporate announcements to public constituencies.

*Informal* speech, the second level of language usage, is marked by a conversational or consultative relationship between the speaker and his or her listeners. Personal pronouns (I, you, and we) are expected. Informal speech may use anecdotes and humor. In business speech, an informal level of language usage is appropriate to almost any situation in which the speaker can anticipate an audience's viewpoint and allows for some explicit or implicit give-and-take.

*Casual* speech is reserved for a close relationship between speaker and listener. This level of usage relies on slang, inside references, and ellipses of information. Not everything has to be spelled out in casual speech because the individuals involved share a common background and viewpoint. Casual speech marks much of family conversation and that of close friendships. In business, it is appropriate only for in-house speech and then only among equals on common ground. The casual level of language usage rarely serves well in public speech.

*Intimate* language, the fourth level, is highly personal, almost visceral. It is bound only by the peculiar grammar of an intimate relationship and, often, has no lexical structure recognizable outside the relationship (e.g., the "conversation" of a parent and newborn baby). By definition, intimate speech is inappropriate to public communication.

Effective business speech tends to rely on the first two levels of language and returns most often to the informal level. A careful analysis of good speech transcripts (and essays) indicates that on a given occasion a speaker may use two levels but never three. That is, a speech may alternate between formal and informal speech, but the same speech ought not to include a casual level of usage, too. Audience expectations allow a speaker to shift levels of language usage but not to jump (i.e., to skip a level).

When studying examples of business communication, whether verbal or written, observe the intimate connections between information and language. Individual words and their combinations into sentences form and break the contracts of implied meaning between a speaker and an audience. The selection of words must be made with a fair view toward representing the speaker's intention and facilitating a listener's perception. Kinds of words must be chosen to depict our logical, sensory, emotional, and imaginative thinking in response to a given issue. And individual words must be blended into a general level of usage that gives shape to and defines an implied relationship between speaker and audience.

The selection of words must be made with a fair view toward representing the speaker's intention and facilitating a listener's perception. Kinds of words must be chosen to depict our logical, sensory, emotional, and imaginative thinking in response to a given issue. And individual words must be blended into a general level of usage that gives shape to and defines an implied relationship between speaker and audience.

## EXERCISES

**A**   Consider the relationship between intention and perception in the following speech assignments. For each situation described below, write one paragraph that satisfies the objective. Compose orally so that your paragraphs will "read" as speech.

1. You are the supervisor of an industrial line. At an assembly of your workers, announce that weekly productivity has declined for seven consecutive weeks as compared with the same period of the year before. Your intention is to motivate greater effort from workers.

2. Present the same information as required in situation #1 above. However, now your intention is to warn workers that personnel changes (i.e., firings) will result if productivity remains low.

3. You are a market analyst making a presentation to corporate executives regarding the geographical distribution of sales. As part of your analysis, you observe that sales in the northeast rose 2 percent in one year. This figure does *not* seem to you significant; therefore, present the percentage in such a way that it will be remembered but not emphasized in the listener's perception.

4. You are again a market analyst assigned to present the information in situation #3 above. Now, however, your intention is to underscore the great significance of a 2 percent increase in sales in the northeast region.

5. You are an interviewer in the personnel department of a large corporation. Report to a job applicant that he or she is unlikely to receive a given appointment but that you will keep the application on file for future consideration. Make the statement in such a way that the concluding words of encouragement will be perceived as genuine.

**B**   Below are described several figures of speech. Learn the definition of each and practice its use by creating examples as assigned. Notice how figurative language conveys information *and* attitude.

1. A *metaphor* is an implied comparison between two unlike things, ascribing features or qualities of one to the other. Whereas a metaphor, if taken literally, is always a lie, its function is to explicate or highlight an embedded meaning in a word or image. Metaphors, if used well, can startle with their informative impact and persuasive appeal, fixing an idea in the listener's mind. If used poorly, without imagination, metaphors can degenerate into lifeless clichés (e.g., "we play hardball here" or "Simpson is a bear of a boss.") An extended metaphor used to control a speech's whole structure is called a *conceit*.

   Two examples of metaphor follow:

   Your organizational chart is a tortuous labyrinth.
   John is a tiger, to be sure, but he's been declawed.

   Compose a metaphor describing each of the following terms:

   a. the MBA degree          _____
   b. the PR specialist       _____
   c. product safety          _____
   d. sales instinct          _____
   e. executive decision making  _____

2. A *simile* is an expressed comparison between two unlike things using the word "like" or "as." An extended simile is called an *analogy*.

   Two examples of simile follow:

   The buzzing on that telephone lines runs through my brain like an electrical shock.
   To go into production without the necessary capital secured is like drawing to an inside straight.

Compose a simile describing each of the following terms:

a. employment interview  _____
b. resumé  _____
c. business reports  _____
d. word processor  _____
e. committee work  _____

3. *Personification* is a use of language that ascribes human qualities to inanimate objects, animals, or abstract ideas.

Two examples of personification follow:

The vice president's office gobbles up the best people and leaves the leftovers for us. That computer just stole my paragraph and won't give it back.

Use personification to describe each of the following terms or ideas:

a. telephone  _____
b. briefcase  _____
c. foreign competition  _____
d. industrial waste  _____
e. corporate profits  _____

4. An *oxymoron* is a figure of speech that forces together antithetical terms. Such a strong contrast can be comic or profound in its insight. In either case, an effective oxymoron should be fun to compose and startling to hear.
Two examples of oxymoron follow:

depressed optimist
eloquent silence

Compose an oxymoron using each of the following terms:

a. fool  _____
b. academic  _____
c. military  _____
d. industrious  _____
e. pragmatist  _____

**C** Over a period of one week, fill in the following record of language that you use, hear, or read. Categorize usage by the headings formal, informal, casual, and intimate. Find at least five examples of speech or writing that typify a given level. Whenever possible, record language usage verbatim. Note, too, the occasion and appropriateness of the language level used.

*One Week's Language Usage*

| | Formal | | | Informal | | |
|---|---|---|---|---|---|---|
| | Example | Occasion | Appropriateness | Example | Occasion | Appropriateness |
| 1 | | | | | | |
| 2 | | | | | | |
| 3 | | | | | | |
| 4 | | | | | | |
| 5 | | | | | | |

*One Week's Language Usage* (con't.)

Casual

Intimate

| | Example | Occasion | Appropriateness | Example | Occasion | Appropriateness |
|---|---|---|---|---|---|---|
| 1 | | | | | | |
| 2 | | | | | | |
| 3 | | | | | | |
| 4 | | | | | | |
| 5 | | | | | | |

## SAMPLE SPEECH

Here is a short address given as part of a college commencement ceremony at which Cecil Burner was given an honorary degree for his contributions to the college. These are the public remarks he made when accepting the honor. When reading the transcript, pay special attention to the function of language in conveying information, projecting personality, and shaping audience perception.

---

Thanks, a million times thanks for this great honor. Thanks to the Board of Trustees, to President Alberts, and the student-faculty selection committee. I'm not going to talk a long time, but I have a few things to say, and I'd appreciate your attention for two minutes.

I never went to college and, frankly, I don't regret that decision. After high school, I needed a job, and my family needed money. I worked for three good companies before founding my own business. While others were studying in the classroom, I was learning on the job. Business has been, for me, the richest classroom around—the best laboratory with the best facilities and the best teachers. The tests have come unannounced, and the grades have never been inflated. I've paid my dues as I've gone along. I've matriculated and graduated time and again in different spheres of the business enterprise. That world is endless—equal, in fact, to all of life.

I know very well why I've been given this honor today. It's not because I deserve an academic degree. The honor is in return for a sum of dollars that I've given to the college. And I'm happy to support higher education. My point today is just to say to you, don't think that your schooling is over when you get this piece of paper.

---

Here is an interesting speech communicating on several dimensions simultaneously. The address begins slowly and ends abruptly. On the simplest level, the speaker expresses gratitude for an honor given and received. On a second level, the speaker seems self-interested as he explains in brief the pattern of his professional development. An integral part of this story is the repeated information that the speaker did not attend college. On still another level, the speaker seems less interested in self and concerned more for the future welfare of the graduating students.

There is, in the speech's diction and syntax, a sense of preparation *and* spontaneity from the speaker. The first two paragraphs seem more prepared than the third. The speech ends in an aggressive verbal gesture to the audience.

## DISCUSSION QUESTIONS

1. From the language and content of this speech, how old would you judge the speaker to be? On what specific evidence do you base your speculation?
2. If you are a graduating senior in the audience and a businessperson is introduced to receive an honorary degree, what immediate assumptions might you make about the person?
3. Evaluate the communication impact of the speaker's references to his not having a college education. What do you take to be the message or multiple messages (conscious or unconscious) of this information?
4. Evaluate the communication effectiveness of the speaker's analogy between a college classroom and education on the job.
5. What are the advantages and disadvantages of the speaker's drawing attention to his financial gift to the college?
6. What do you take to be the speaker's attitudes toward himself, toward the audience, and toward the occasion throughout this speech? Do these attitudes seem to change as the speech progresses? Specifically, what implied attitudes on the part of the speaker inform your understanding of the final paragraph? Can the language bear more than one legitimate reading?

## HYPOTHETICAL SPEECHES

Imagine the situation of a corporation with one of its three divisions that designs software under government contract. At the end of a given contract, management receives word that a new contract will not be granted due to government cutbacks. Your assignment is to announce this loss to various constituencies of the corporation. Compose three one-paragraph speeches. The first should be directed to shareholders and should be delivered in formal language. The second situation asks for a speech to all corporate employees and should use informal language. The third situation places you in the role of a division manager addressing the employees who have worked together for a number of years on this government contract and who will be personally affected by the loss. Deliver this speech on the casual level of language usage.

Write all three speech paragraphs. Then discuss as a class the appropriateness of language usage given the variables of topic and audience.

## SUMMARY

The reporting of information in business speech depends greatly upon a speaker's use of language. Words are not inert containers of meaning but are dynamic conveyors of intention and perception. They must be chosen with care to project fully a speaker's perspective while, at the same time, protecting and ensuring the accurate perception of a listener. Meaning, ultimately, is a stock jointly held by speaker and audience, and neither party alone has power to ascribe meaning without the concurrence of the other.

A good speaker develops and draws upon a deep, rich vocabulary. The active inventory of words available to a business speaker must include technical terminology, as well as language suitable to a nonexpert. The broader and more current one's working vocabulary is, the more topics and audiences one may address with effect. At a minimum, any speaker should be able to use words of declaration, imagery, and figurative language. One's goal always is to find the *best* word to describe a given idea, a way of thinking, an attitude, or a feeling and the one most likely to be remembered by an audience as fresh and striking in its insight and efficiency.

Typical language usage can be categorized on four levels. Formal speech is appropriate to high pronouncements requiring no specific relationship between speaker and audience. Informal speech, by its diction and structure, offers the listener a conversational or consultative relationship with the speaker. The casual level of language usage is reserved for "insiders" and is marked by slang and ellipses of information. Intimate language, then, describes highly personal, idiosyncratic grammar unique to an intimate relationship — inappropriate to a public occasion. Business speech relies most upon the formal and informal levels of language with careful use of the casual level for in-house occasions among equals. The advantage of informal language usage, that level recommended for most public speaking situations, is its expectation of an explicit relationship between speaker and audience.

# 10

# The Text: Persuasion and Structure

Structure is a critical term covering, finally, all of a text's dimensions. For our purposes, however, the term refers especially to the sequence of speech parts, an ordering that provides discernible shape to discourse. In previous chapters, we have talked about intention and perception, voice and viewpoint, information and language. Discussion here centers on some principles of structure in a speech text and the impact of sequencing on persuasion.

## PRINCIPLES OF STRUCTURE

To understand the communication principles underlying a speech structure, one must first dismiss any definitions of the term limiting its range and significance. While structure involves sequence, it is not merely organizational. Whereas the term implies spatial perception, it includes temporal movement as well. The connotations of "structure" evoke unfortunate mechanistic images, unfortunate because the term is person-centered. Speech structure links person and thought, person and person, person and language, person and environment. Structure is, from start to finish, a manifestation of the speaker's person and an appeal to the listener's person.

A satisfying speech structure provides direction and impetus to the speaker's intention. It also facilitates a listener's perception by grouping items of information into meaningful and memorable patterns. In addition to serving its speaker and servicing its audience, a satisfying speech structure creates a kind of autonomy for the text as a thing in itself. If that structure is firm—uniquely crafted by the material—the speech text will take on an apparent life of its own. When one understands fully the value of structure, one recognizes its essential connections to all components of a speech act. A good structure defines and validates the relationship among speaker, audience, and text. The general principles that guide proper structuring grow out of these three accountabilities.

A speech structure must project accurately the thought and viewpoint of a speaker.

This mandate implies that language alone is not a sufficient conveyor of a speaker's intention. As important as diction is, words are understood within a given context, which helps to determine the meanings of those words. The speaker can provide a reliable context by sequencing information in a pattern that reflects his or her priorities and values. The points at which a speaker chooses to begin and to end a speech *say* something about his or her attitudes toward the topic and the audience. The critical turning points in a speaker's argument and the kinds of appeals that it makes *say* something about the speaker's viewpoint. The length of time devoted to each part of a speech *says* something about the speaker's intention. And the juxtaposition of topics within a speech *says* something about the speaker's thought processes. Each of these structural variables (beginning and ending, transitions, duration, and juxtaposition) should serve to underscore a speaker's intention, to project accurately his or her position and attitude toward a given topic.

A speech structure must guide the spatial and temporal perceptions of an audience.

The second mandate takes into account the obligations of structure to a listener. All along we have maintained that communication strategies must be designed to meet the needs of both speaker and audience. Consideration of one without the other *cannot* enhance communication between the two. Each structural variable should be linked to knowledge of the audience and a sharing of their collective viewpoint by the speaker. Hence, the choices of where to begin and end a speech should be based, in part, upon the interests, prior knowledge, and anticipated response of an audience. Transitions must move the audience efficiently through time from one point to the next while guarding a listener's accumulated perceptions of meaning. The amount of time given to each speech topic and the particular juxtaposition of subjects must also be predicated upon listener needs.

A speech structure must provide organic identity to a text.

This third mandate accords to a speech text the prerogatives of its own identity. Whereas speeches are temporal acts given shape by a particular occasion, a specific speaker, and a certain audience, the words of a speech can transcend their environment and take on an apparent life form independent of speaker and audience. There is nothing very mysterious in this transformation. It is commonplace to remember a line from a speech, an anecdote, an example, or even the structure of a whole argument while forgetting *who* said it or *when* and *where* it was said. In this instance, a speech takes on its own life. To an extent, this ascribing of independence to a speech text or any of its parts may be a measure of its communicative success. The fundamental principle underlying textual independence is organic identity. This means that a speech structure is *natural* to its topic. It must exhibit a skeleton, a musculature, and a complexion that fit together into an organic whole, alive and indivisible. The structure of a speech text, while consciously crafted by its speaker, cannot be arbitrarily imposed; it must evolve naturally from the materials of the speech (i.e., thought, feeling, and attitude).

## STRATEGIES OF PERSUASION

The purposes of human speech are nearly limitless: to inform, to tease, to express feelings, to confess, to give comfort, to argue, to defend, to attack, to negotiate, to arouse, and to appease, to name only a few. The purposes of public speech, while filling a somewhat narrower range than all human communication, are many and various. The examples and cases offered in this book alone suggest an array of rhetorical aims within the confines of business speech. It is necessary to bear in mind the vastness of public speech so that we don't overgeneralize its definition. If one reflects on the numbers and types of speeches in the world of commerce, the various constituencies that they represent, the profiles of possible audiences, and the catalog of conceivable topics, the practitioner of business speech assumes a proper modesty (even more so, the would-be critic or teacher of public speaking).

One must be especially wary of oversimplification when discussing the possible structures of business speech. If one were to accept the word of every self-help manual, one could collect a sizeable number of magical formulas for delivering "sure-fire" speeches. But the point of making a serious study of business rhetoric is to assert that the speech event is always unique, always richly complicated, always multidimensional. No simple formula can predict success for every speaker, every topic, and every occasion. At best, we can learn some basic principles that will help to determine communicative potential in a given public speaking situation.

*Most* business speeches are delivered to affect some specific change in the audience. When the listener is known to be antagonistic toward a topic, the speaker's aim is *to reduce* that resistance. When the listener is known to be apathetic toward a topic, the speaker's aim is *to arouse* interest. In the case of an audience with a mild interest, the purpose is *to activate* greater enthusiasm and commitment. For an audience already deeply committed in principle, the speaker's aim is *to actuate* a plan of action. When a speaker and an audience already are working together toward a common goal, the aim of a public speech is *to affirm* that commonality, thereby strengthening further the kindred bonds. Each of these speech aims (to reduce resistance, to arouse interest, to activate commitment, to actuate action, and to affirm a common goal) implies change. Each one also implies communication links among speaker, audience, and text.

A speaker's task is to guide the process of change by sensible, efficient, and ethical means of persuasion. Lasting change in an audience's opinions, beliefs, attitudes, or actions must come about through their own free choice—a fact acknowledged and appreciated by any good speaker. Lasting change cannot be coerced. (Short-term persuasion *can* be affected by a speaker's unethical tactics of threatening, bribing, misquoting, lying, or withholding of vital information. Such strategies are guaranteed to double back on their users with fatal consequences to future communications.) To recognize and affirm a listener's free choice does not reduce the tools for persuasion available to a public speaker. Rather, one is free to argue a viewpoint with all the vigor and persuasive skills one can muster as long as the freedom to respond is permitted to an audience.

If the aim of most business speeches is to affect specific change in an audience's opinions, beliefs, attitudes, or actions, the place to begin shaping an efficient structure is at the end. As seen earlier, speech perception occurs over time. To persuade a listener of the validity of any viewpoint, one must project oneself into the desired perspective and work backwards through time to analyze the changes required to adopt that perspective. Unless a speaker can specify the end response desired of an audience and can analyze accurately their probable perceptions at the beginning of a speech, persuasion is nearly impossible. A speaker must learn to lead an audience step by step through a logical argument, moment by moment through a telling example, and number by number through a difficult equation.

The generic outline for a persuasive speech has five parts, usually presented in the following order:

1. Introduction (with the purpose of gaining and focusing attention)
2. Thesis (with the purpose of declaring a speaker's position)
3. Definitions (with the purpose of ensuring a common understanding of key terms)
4. Development (with the purpose of explaining, explicating, expanding, exemplifying, or defending the thesis)
5. Conclusion (with the double purpose of summarizing and calling for a desired response)

This generic outline, like the inexpensive and simply labeled groceries, is basic— unadorned by rhetorical features. Myriad changes and embellishments are possible. Nevertheless, this outline includes the essential components of a speech text.

The best way to increase one's own repertoire of rhetorical strategies is to observe carefully all samples of public speech—whether witnessed in person, via television, by radio, or in printed transcript. A good speaker, always alert for new ways to organize a text, should keep a work journal describing and evaluating speeches heard or read. In this journal, one should note all aspects of the speech event that we have discussed (e.g., language, perception, time, environment, voice, delivery, and information). Record observations of structure by noting the sequence of major shifts in a speech's argument and especially the overall pattern by which individual parts grow together.

There are numerous patterns by which persuasive speeches may be structured. To begin your own list, here are five typical approaches:

## List of Reasons

In this pattern, a speaker defends his or her thesis simply by listing the reasons why an audience ought to consider and adopt the product, idea, or viewpoint. Such an approach may be most effective for topics that an audience did not know previously and that do not compete with opposing positions.

## Comparative Advantages

In situations where there are two or more perspectives toward a given subject (or two or more products competing for the same market), the speaker may choose a structure of comparative advantages. Based on a classical debate strategy, this approach acknowledges openly that more than one viewpoint (or product) is acceptable but that the speaker's position is preferable to all others. With this structure, one lists the advantages of each alternative and shows how and why one's own position is better than competing ones.

## Negative Method

An approach nearly opposite to comparative advantages is the negative method. Here, rather than acknowledge the viability of many viewpoints, one argues that all positions available toward a given issue are flawed. By going through a list of alternative viewpoints one at a time and illustrating the shortcomings of each, one is finally left with only one position—that advocated by the speaker.

## Problem-Solution

This conventional structure for persuasion might also be termed need-fulfillment. This speaker's appeal to the audience rests entirely upon their perception of a problem and the need for a solution. Until a listener can be persuaded that the problem exists and is serious enough to warrant action, no solution will win endorsement. After establishing the scope and significance of a problem, this speaker is obliged to show how his or her solution meets the specific demands of the situation.

## Criteria Satisfaction

Here is a particularly appealing, though difficult, approach to a sales speech. This speaker advocates a given product or position by first outlining criteria by which excellence may be measured. These standards, to be effective, must be objective, measurable, and (whenever possible) endorsed by a professional agency or association. If such criteria for excellence can be established, a speaker then proceeds to explain or demonstrate how a given product or viewpoint matches each criterion and, thus, achieves excellence in the perceptions of an audience.

These are but five rhetorical strategies for moving an audience through reasoned change. Many others exist. Speech is a highly pragmatic art. Results are not measured by a speaker's adherence to formula but by the real communication achieved with an audience. An approach appropriate to one topic and audience may be entirely inappropriate to another subject or another audience. Do not be restricted by these or other strategies for speech. Rather, apply common sense and basic principles of public communication to the analysis of a given speech assignment, and customize an approach most suitable to that occasion.

## SOME STRUCTURAL GUIDELINES

The study of speech structures can become richly complicated, and generalizations take one only so far. The most practical learning occurs in the analysis of specific speech texts and their contexts—human, environmental, and commercial. In the second part of this book, we shall return to structural considerations in the preparation of eight types of typical business speeches. At this introductory stage, however, five specific guidelines to speech structuring are delineated.

First, test the logical validity of a speech's structure as the expression of reasoned argument. Do not assume that effective delivery, language, or information alone can substitute for a logical pattern unifying the whole speech.

Second, check a speech text to be sure that an audience will make any perceptual jump that is not clearly indicated in the speech itself. Like a proofreader who unconsciously fills in gaps and corrects errors in a manuscript, many speakers are prone to supply the missing links of an argument by their own mental processes without specifying these to an audience. This lapse of consciousness in the preparation or delivery of a speech is always detrimental to communication and persuasion.

Third, expect *reasonable* change in an audience's position toward a topic. Do not expect to move a listener too far in one speech. Remember that a given address may fit into a pattern of persuasive appeals extending beyond the public speaking situation. The more firmly held a listener's predisposition is, the less change may be anticipated. An argument must be most compelling to affect a change of belief.

Fourth, take care to integrate all quotations or statistical references into the speech text as a whole. A speaker is obliged to make the necessary transitions in and out of quoted material and to illustrate its relevance to the developing structural pattern. When using an outside authority to supplement one's own presentation, a speaker serves as a kind of narrator introducing and controlling the use and impact of that resource.

Fifth, be sure that a speech's structure makes room for all important information without extraneous appendages. An effective structure evolves naturally from a speech's materials, and one of the measures of its success is economy of expression. If certain items of importance do not fit neatly into the categories of a given structure, the speaker should search farther for a more appropriate pattern.

These guidelines may serve as a checklist for speech preparation and as a standard of measure in evaluating speech structures. As you develop expertise in shaping persuasive speeches, you may care to expand the list to include other recommendations for structural excellence.

## THE SATISFACTIONS OF STRUCTURE

A good speech structure, like language well used, offers unique satisfactions to the speaker and listener. To fashion a logical argument that holds together from beginning to end offers real pleasure to any orator and places a business speaker in the company of philosophers and statesmen throughout history. To move people by the appeal of reasoned words rather than by the force of might or position is in itself a civilizing process. The impetus and impact of reason are carried largely by the shape of discourse, by structure. Structure also satisfies with its mnemonic value. It provides a memorable record of a journey taken and marks with special interest all turns along the way to a destination. Like the pleasures of an artfully crafted beginning, middle, and end of a novel, the structure of a good speech validates itself with aesthetic economy and everyday common sense. Structure, more than any other textual dimension, is a perception shared between speaker and audience. The perceived shape of a speech prescribes the common ground on which a speaker and his or her listener may meet, converse, negotiate, argue, and settle differences. When that structure provides a large enough ground to accommodate both parties and a fair enough vista to encourage free exchange, the probability of reasoned change is great.

## EXERCISES

**A**   Over the next two weeks, keep a speech journal observing the structural patterns of five public speeches. You may include in your survey any business speech, formal lecture, sermon, televised presidential address, or other public speech. If you cannot attend five speeches or view them on TV, you may read the complete transcripts of speeches as recorded in major daily newspapers (e.g., *The New York Times*). Use the following forms to record your observations.

*Speech Journal #1*

Date: _____

Speaker: _____

Title of speech (if available): _____

Occasion: _____


What is the speaker's apparent thesis?


Describe the speech's structure. Specify the sequence of major parts, and describe the unifying pattern of the whole.


Evaluate the communication merits and demerits of this structure. Defend its positive points and recommend revisions for its negative aspects.

*Speech Journal #2*

Date: _____

Speaker: _____

Title of speech (if available): _____

Occasion: _____


What is the speaker's apparent thesis?


Describe the speech's structure. Specify the sequence of major parts, and describe the unifying pattern of the whole.


Evaluate the communication merits and demerits of this structure. Defend its positive points and recommend revisions for its negative aspects.

*Speech Journal #3*

Date: _____

Speaker: _____

Title of speech (if available): _____

Occasion: _____

What is the speaker's apparent thesis?

Describe the speech's structure. Specify the sequence of major parts, and describe the unifying pattern of the whole.

Evaluate the communication merits and demerits of this structure. Defend its positive points and recommend revisions for its negative aspects.

*Speech Journal #4*

Date: _____

Speaker: _____

Title of speech (if available): _____

Occasion: _____


What is the speaker's apparent thesis?




Describe the speech's structure. Specify the sequence of major parts, and describe the unifying pattern of the whole.




Evaluate the communication merits and demerits of this structure. Defend its positive points and recommend revisions for its negative aspects.

*Speech Journal #5*

Date: _____

Speaker: _____

Title of speech (if available): _____

Occasion: _____

What is the speaker's apparent thesis?

Describe the speech's structure. Specify the sequence of major parts, and describe the unifying pattern of the whole.

Evaluate the communication merits and demerits of this structure. Defend its positive points and recommend revisions for its negative aspects.

**B**   Suggest three speech topics for which each of the following structures may be appropriate. Then, as a class, compare your suggestions, and discuss the criteria by which appropriateness may be determined.

    1. List of Reasons
        a.

        b.

        c.

    2. Comparative Advantages
        a.

      b.

      c.

3. Negative Method
    a.

      b.

c.

4. Problem-Solution
   a.

   b.

   c.

5. Criteria Satisfaction
   a.



   b.



   c.



C  Prepare a three-minute speech to sell your audience on a favorite movie (or book) released within the last year. Use the rhetorical approach of criteria satisfaction by listing first the hallmarks of an excellent movie (or book) and then showing how your selection meets those standards. Use the following worksheet to help prepare the speech text.

1. List below in arbitrary order all the qualities of excellence that you look for in a good film (or book):

   _____
   _____
   _____
   _____
   _____
   _____
   _____
   _____
   _____
   _____
   _____

2. Study the list above and draw together any qualities that may be linked under a common heading.

3. Number the criteria in your shortened list from most to least important.

4. List three good movies (or books) that you have seen in the past year.

   _____

   _____

   _____

5. Measure each selection against your critical criteria.

6. Which movie seems to embody most your standards of excellence?

   _____

7. Select three criteria that you consider most compelling because of their applicability to the movie (or book) you have chosen.

8. Select a specific scene, character, or other feature in the film (or book) that exemplifies each criterion.

9. Outline the speech below. Be sure to include your critical criteria early on in the text's development. Be specific in reference to the film (or book). Choose carefully the point at which you name the title of the movie (or book).

**D**  List below five beliefs or opinions that you hold with such conviction that no speech could persuade you to think otherwise.

    1.

    2.

    3.

    4.

5.

## SAMPLE SPEECH

Here is a brief speech delivered as part of the introductory session of a six-week seminar for graduate students in English who are in the process of choosing business careers. The address had three aims: (1) to introduce its speaker, a public relations executive, (2) to introduce the students to a business world not entirely unlike their backgrounds in literature, and (3) to introduce a paradigm for envisioning corporate structure.

Good morning, ladies and gentlemen, and let me add my words of welcome to those already given. In the weeks to come, you will be indoctrinated into the ways of commerce, and for many of you this shift in career must seem like a cataclysmic upheaval of all that you've prepared yourself for in the liberal arts, especially those of you with backgrounds in literature. Many of you, in the application forms, indicated a special interest in the field of public relations as a point of entry into business. No doubt, you figured that PR specialists, like English majors, spend their days with words, and this at least appeared a familiar skill. You would not be entirely wrong in that assumption, but if your thinking has gone no further than that, you've stopped at an elementary level. The overlap between literary analysis and the work of public relations is broad, and the practice of PR will call on all the ingenuity required of a crack literary critic.

Picture, if you will, a corporate structure as the world of a novel and its external constituencies—shareholders, consumers, and competitors—as readers. This analogy is no superficial gloss: it suggests some startling parallels. A corporation, like a novel, is a highly structured world peopled by characters of every description and upheld by underlying themes. The plots of both worlds are enacted in space and time settings that themselves give meaning to characters and their actions. Both worlds mark their development by conflict, crises, climaxes, and resolutions.

The similarity that I want you to consider is the all-important function of a narrator in both a novel and a corporation. You know better than I how a narrator functions in a novel to control reader perception. The narrator stands as a kind of liason between the fictional world where characters exist and the real world of the reader. The narrator metes out information to the reader in such a way that the novel's action will make sense and become memorable. The narrator can alter the pace of that telling by summary or description. He can define a point of view by which meaning may be interpreted. And he ultimately is the one to give shape or structure to the novel's world in the reader's mind.

Well, I'm here to tell you that the public relations specialist is a corporation's narrator. He or she shapes perception by meting out information, controlling the pace of action, and interpreting the meaning of events. Ultimately, it is the PR specialist who gives structure to a business enterprise in the world's mind.

Think about that. When you come into our classrooms during the next six weeks, do not leave behind you all that you've learned as though it were useless baggage in this new world. We need you *and* your backgrounds. You'll find that if you've a mind for application, your study of literature will stand you in good stead as a foundation for understanding a business system.

One can only speculate on the responses of an audience to this speech. For a listener who had not considered carefully the possible links between English studies and business activities, the speech might prompt a real change of attitude. This speaker attains his three objectives by the rhetorical strategy of an analogy. Comparing a corporation to a novel, external constituencies to readers, and the PR specialist to a narrator shows tangible links between the backgrounds of this audience and the business expertise of the speaker. By helping the listeners to make one set of connections between worlds, the speaker encourages the audience to continue the effort. Perhaps more important than this intellectual challenge, the speech text is likely to evoke attitudinal change. An audience of English graduates would certainly warm to a business executive coming to their literary turf—a communication decision likely to break down some resistance or negative preconceptions that a student of literature may have about the world of commerce. Interestingly, for our purposes, the speech is all about structures, as well—the structures of a novel and a corporation, and the structure of a persuasive analogy.

## DISCUSSION QUESTIONS

1. What assumptions has the speaker made about the identity, knowledge, and attitudes of this audience? Support your answers with specific references to the speech text.
2. Of what communication value in this context are such word choices as "cataclysmic upheaval," "indoctrinated," "literary analysis," and "reader perception"?
3. Discuss the values of this speaker's analogy. What other similarities might be explored between the function of a narrator and that of a PR specialist? What differences between a novel and a corporation exist that might undermine the validity of this analogy?
4. Evaluate the communication effectiveness of this speech structure in terms of its apparent persuasive aims.

## HYPOTHETICAL SPEECH

Deliver a ten-minute persuasive speech regarding government regulation of American industry. Select one industry (e.g., banking, airlines, farming), describe the current state of government regulation, and advocate a specific change — either increased regulation or deregulation. This speech will require research. You may need to narrow the subject to a specific sector of an industry. Structure your ten minutes with a persuasive pattern that will present a viewpoint sensibly and with memorable impact on the audience.

## SUMMARY

The structure of a speech text, its overall shape, is the sum of all parts and depends especially on the relationships among parts — their sequence, duration, and transitional links. A speech structure that does its job well can project a speaker's thought and viewpoint while guiding the perceptions of an audience and providing organic identity for the text itself. The structure of a speech can be crafted and controlled by the speaker, to a certain extent. However, structure must grow naturally from the speech materials themselves and cannot be imposed arbitrarily on an inappropriate topic or audience.

Speech structures, especially in a commercial context, are related intimately to a process of persuasion. *Most* business speeches are delivered to affect a specific change in an audience's opinion, attitude, belief, or behavior. Depending upon the relative distance between a speaker's viewpoint and that of his or her audience, the persuasive aim differs (e.g., to reduce resistance, to arouse interest, to activate deeper commitment, to actuate a plan of action, or to affirm a commonly held perspective). A speaker's mandate is to guide this process of change by sensible, efficient, and ethical means of persuasion. The overall shape of a speech, with its sequence of information and its gradual revelation of viewpoint, reflects a speaker's attitudes toward the topic and the audience. Several rhetorical strategies are available for structuring persuasive arguments. Five conventional approaches are a list of reasons, comparative advantages, the negative method, problem-solution, and criteria satisfaction.

As an introduction to the study of speech structures, test your own practice by these five guidelines:

1. Does the speech structure give a vaild expression to a logical argument?
2. Does the structure specify each step in a sequence of desired change?
3. Does the structure expect reasonable change from the audience?
4. Does the structure allow for the integration of outside references (e.g., quotations or statistics) into the speaker's own presentation?
5. Does the basic structure house all information vital to the topic?

A satisfying speech structure meets the expressive and persuasive needs of a speaker. It also facilitates the perceptual needs of a listener and protects his or her freedom of thought and response. There is even a link between organizational competence and a speaker's overcoming communication anxiety or apprehension—so potent is the function of structure to the whole speech process.

    With this consideration of structure, we conclude the introduction of textual matters. Through the past nine chapters, we have looked at how the speaker, the audience, and the text each contribute to the dynamic gestalt of speech communication. In Chapter 14, a philosophical overview will be offered before proceeding to the practice of specific speech types. However, there are special topics that transcend our analytical categories that must be considered in a study of business speech. In the next three chapters, we shall look at convention planning, ghost-writing, and the speech in print.

# 11

# Special Consideration: Convention Planning

The potential for communication in a given speech is determined in part by the context of its delivery. A typical business context yielding extraordinary effects is the convention. This setting provides a kind of superstructure for public speaking by being itself a massive speech event. Here, the audience gathers for a stated purpose and listens to the public address of many speakers. Yet within this broad definition are a large range of formats and expectations. A catalog of typical business conventions would have to include the purposes of information exchange, continuing education, job training, problem solving, sales, and policy formulation. Even the number of words used to describe a convention indicates its importance to a business enterprise — conference, symposium, meeting, forum, seminar. In this chapter, we look at the typical formats of a convention, objectives and planning, and the role of a convention director.

## CONVENTION FORMATS

Three basic formats describe most business activity in the convention setting: general assembly, small group, and panel. All three formats may be used for the purposes of a given convention or one may suffice to meet the objective. Our aim is not to analyze in detail the dynamics of a business convention but to discuss generally the significance of various formats on speech preparation and delivery.

The *general assembly* is a staple of most conventions, convened at the beginning and the end or, on occasion, serving as the sole format. Here all convention participants gather to hear one speaker or a succession of several. The number of those attending a typical business convention ranges from fifty to over a thousand. The size of such an audience suggests certain constraints and certain possibilities for a speaker. The physical setup itself confers authority upon each speaker. An elevated rostrum or podium, special lighting, and microphones are all agents of focus and control for one who knows how to use them. At the same time, the setup of a general assembly diminishes a speaker's control by creating distance from an audience and reducing the effectiveness of physical or vocal nuance.

When called upon to address such a large audience, a speaker should learn as much as possible beforehand about the setting. The more details of a situation one knows, the more control one may exert over communication and, interestingly, over oneself. Find out, for instance, when on the program you are to speak, where you are to await your turn, and what to do after your speech (i.e., when to leave the platform and where to go). If possible, rehearse under the lights, assessing the size and feel of a phantom audience and checking your notes or manuscript for any troublesome glare. It is essential, as well, that microphones be tested, appropriate sound levels set, and full instructions be given by a sound technician regarding the flexibility of a given public address system. Ask how far to stand from a microphone, how far you can walk away in each direction without losing volume, and, if using a lapel or lavaliere mike, how to fasten and unfasten it. Check all sight lines from the audience to determine the best place to set up visual aids. Finally, rehearse a speech in the actual setting, whenever possible. Feel the size of gesture and voice that the space requires. When rehearsal in the actual setting is impossible, be sure to animate your private practice (even in the confines of a hotel room) with the imagined projection of a large audience. The format of a general assembly not only affects speech delivery: it affects all textual choices. As the size of an audience increases, the speaker takes on greater obligations to choose a vocabulary, a style, a structure, and all examples with a view toward the interests and backgrounds of a large public.

The *small group* format provides a somewhat simpler, or at least more familiar, setting for most business speakers. A convention organized as a series of small group sessions, often with several meeting at the same time, recognizes the special needs and interests of individual constituencies within the larger body of a general assembly. Usually the participants in a given group have selected a particular session from a printed program or have been assigned to attend because of the special relevance of a session to an individual's work. There are many ways of organizing small group sessions. One approach calls for a series of presentations by speakers, with a moderator introducing and summarizing the whole session. Another calls for the formal presentation of one or more papers, with the rebuttal or critique of a respondent. Still another approach allows questions and answers from the audience at the end of a presentation. Most often, the small group session is organized as an informal classroom, with give and take between a speaker and the audience in the form of questions or participatory exercises.

When speaking in a small group session, one must consider several variables that are unique to the convention context. First, one should determine the contribution of a given session to the objectives of the whole convention. A successful small group is not isolated from the larger setting but is integral to the overall communication scheme. Second, in a group with more than one speaker, each participant must help ensure that his or her presentation fits into the pattern of the others, so that the session as a whole will make sense. Third, a speaker in a small group setting may assume greater homogeneity of knowledge and interest among audience members than in the setting of a general assembly. As in all other public speaking situations, practical advantages accrue to one who can forecast accurately the perspectives of listeners.

A *panel* format is distinctive for its group presentation. Again the physical setup, usually a table with chairs or a series of lecterns, prescribes communication patterns to some extent. Panelists are equals, each contributing a different viewpoint to the explication of a common theme. While formal speeches are occasionally delivered by panel members, the more usual practice is for each speaker to offer brief remarks prepared in advance. Then a moderator orchestrates further discussion among panelists or with the audience.

When invited to speak on a panel, one should consider carefully the context. A clear theme or question must be kept central to the panel's discussion, and each member is responsible for ensuring that centrality. Good panels, well chosen and well led, offer a diversity of viewpoints. Each member ought to think out his or her perspective in detail before participating. The apparently free-for-all atmosphere of panel discussions spiced with wit or barbed with sarcasm should not deceive one about their nature. A good panelist prepares ahead, comes to the occasion with evidence in support of his or her viewpoint, and, most importantly, is prepared to listen actively to others. These preparations, on occasion, take the form of rigorous rehearsal of likely questions and possible answers.[1]

By introducing the three convention formats—general assembly, small group, and panel—we simply underscore a theme running the length of this study. Public communication is *not* a matter of the speaker's intention alone. Real communication in a public forum also depends upon the perceptions of an audience and the constraints of a given context. When speaking at a business convention, regardless of its purpose, one must consider the effects upon communication of this enlarged speech setting.

## OBJECTIVES AND PLANNING

A convention, like an individual speech, should take shape in response to clear and reasonable objectives. Like the aims of an individual speech, such objectives should be seen and stated from an audience perspective: what specifically may participants expect to get from attending this convention? What should they come away with? Convention

---

[1] An especially interesting look at the preparation of corporate executives for the question-answer period of an annual meeting of shareholders is provided by Sonny Kleinfield in *The Biggest Company on Earth: A Profile of AT&T* (New York: Holt, Rinehart and Winston, 1981). See pages 185-199.

planning, then, involves audience analysis and the development of communication strategies for moving participants from their probable starting points to a desired end. Planning a convention is like planning a speech on a large scale.

The first step in planning is to state objectives. If it is a sales conference, the aims must be stated as specific goals (e.g., to achieve a certain number of orders or to recruit a certain number of new franchises). If it is a training conference, the aims should be outlined like those of an educational curriculum with specific learning and behavioral objectives (e.g., by the end of this session, participants should know these things and should be able to use these skills). If it is a research symposium, the aims should be stated in terms of theoretical questions to be addressed by all participants. A convention, like a speech, must have a central theme that is clear to the convention organizers *and* clear to the participants. As with a speech, the planner's intention has zero or negative value until it matches the participant's perceptions.

After stating objectives, the second step of convention planning is selecting participants. This stage breaks down into two tasks—choosing the program speakers and inviting the right audience. Both amount to a speaker's responsibility to garner the best available resources to address a given theme. Program speakers are selected by invitation or competition, and their acceptance should be confirmed with as much lead time before the convention as possible. All aspects of individual speech assignments must be outlined clearly (e.g., purpose, length, format, and schedule). Descriptive titles and brief abstracts of all addresses are submitted to the organizer for publication in a convention program. As important to the success of a conference as the quality of speakers is the quality of an audience. The right constituencies must be invited, and they must have ample time to make their plans to attend. In addition, convention programs should provide a descriptive catalog of all opportunities available so that, by self-selection, the best audiences convene for appropriate sessions.

After choosing a convention theme and breaking it down into specific objectives, and after selecting the speakers and inviting an audience, planning continues through numerous questions of logistics. Accommodations for conferees must be arranged, preferably at the actual convention site. Conference facilities must be selected and monitored. It is especially important to check the suitability of each room or auditorium to the purposes of a given session. Adequate seating (number and arrangement) must be available, and the necessary support material on hand (e.g., lectern, microphone, chalkboard, slide projector, easel, overhead projector or other aid requested by the speakers). Facilities management is a subject outside the scope of our study except to remind a convention organizer that all decisions will affect the communicative potential of public address. Speakers are well advised to double check the adequacy of facilities for their sessions upon arrival at a convention site.

## THE ROLE OF A DIRECTOR

One special responsibility of a convention organizer is scheduling, and the topic deserves close attention. Nothing is more critical to the success of a convention than the proper use of time. This demands, at the outset, a master schedule with ample time allowed for the purposes of each session and adequate time for audience movement between sessions. Conference participants expect to attend several meetings in one day, and an organizer may schedule six to eight hours of actual meeting times per day. Because conference participation is a tiring process, coffee and meal breaks must be considered as carefully as scheduling of meetings.

When allocating times for a business convention, an organizer is really an orchestrator or, to use another metaphor, a theatrical producer. One must consider the impact of placing particular sessions in serial order (juxtaposition) or opposite one another (simultaneity). It is especially important to consider the serial structure of the convention as a whole. The sequence of sessions, in itself, becomes part of the meaning perceived by conferees. The effectiveness of a convention can be undermined by careless scheduling, even if individual sessions are very good. The allocation of time slots and the sequencing of sessions should be in the hands of one director, someone who can impose sensible order and make of diverse activities a thematic pattern, itself suggesting meaning. Some corporations are finding the role of convention director so important that executive positions have been created with sole responsibility for conference planning.

The efficient organization of a convention demands some control of persons, facilities, and time. Here are three forms designed for the management of information: a facilities questionnaire, a title and abstract form, and a program page form.

---

### *Facilities Questionnaire*

Part I [to be filled out by organizer]

Name: _____

Program: _____

Date: _____

Time: _____

Room: _____

Part II [to be filled out by speaker]

1. Check (√) below any audio-visual aid required for your presentation:
   _____ audio tape recorder/player
   _____ chalkboard
   _____ easel
   _____ flip pad
   _____ lectern

\_\_\_\_\_ movie projector
\_\_\_\_\_ opaque projector
\_\_\_\_\_ overhead projector
\_\_\_\_\_ pointer
\_\_\_\_\_ screen
\_\_\_\_\_ slide projector (specify kind _____)
\_\_\_\_\_ VTR

2. Specify any other facilities required for your presentation including special seating or room arrangement.

3. List below any special equipment that you will bring with you for use in the presentation.

4. Will an audio-visual operator be required for any of the above equipment? Specify.

Return this form to _____Name_____ by \_\_\_\_Date\_\_\_\_ . Written confirmation of facility requests will be sent to you prior to the convention.

*Title and Abstract Form*

Part I [to be filled out by organizer]

    Date: _____
    Time: _____
    Room: _____

Part II [to be filled out by session moderator or sponsor]

    Program title: _____
    Program moderator: _____

Type below in program sequence the title of each presentation, the name and affiliation of each speaker, and provide a one-paragraph description of each presentation.

    Title: _____
    Speaker: _____ Affiliation: _____

*Abstract*

    Title: _____
    Speaker: _____ Affiliation: _____

*Abstract*

    Return this form to \_\_\_\_\_Name\_\_\_\_\_ by \_\_\_Date\_\_\_.

Program Page Form

## PROGRAM TITLE

_____Time_____                                    _____Room_____

_____Name_____, Moderator

_____Affiliation_____

One-paragraph program description

Speakers:

| | | | | |
|--|--|--|--|--|
| " | Title | ," | Speaker's Name, | Affiliation. |
| " | Title | ," | Speaker's Name, | Affiliation. |
| " | Title | ," | Speaker's Name, | Affiliation. |

## EXERCISES

**A**   In the left-hand column, list ten kinds of business conventions, each requiring a full day or more of meetings. In the right-hand column, identify the major constituency group or groups for whom the convention is planned.

|  | *Kind of Convention* | *Constituency* |
|--|--|--|
| 1. | | |
| 2. | | |
| 3. | | |
| 4. | | |
| 5. | | |
| 6. | | |
| 7. | | |
| 8. | | |
| 9. | | |
| 10. | | |

**B**   Think about the performance and perception differences implied by the three convention formats—general assembly, small group, and panel—and answer the following questions with one-page essay for each.

1. What is the impact upon audience perception when a speaker addresses a large audience from an elevated platform with a darkened auditorium and a well-lit stage? Consider both helpful and harmful effects upon credibility and persuasion under these circumstances.

2. Devise an analogy for the speaker's role in each convention format:

  Speaking before a general assembly is like...

  Speaking in a small group session is like...

  Speaking on a panel is like...

Explicate these analogies and the differences that they imply about formats for business speaking.

3. Devise an analogy for the listener's role in each convention format:

  Attending a general assembly is like...

  Participating in a small group session is like...

  Hearing a panel discussion is like...

Explicate these analogies and the differences that they imply about audience perception in various convention formats.

4. What are the likely differences of perception between attending a speech in person and seeing the same speech on film or TV?

## SAMPLE SPEECH

The annual meeting of shareholders for a publicly held corporation is a special kind of general assembly. Presided over by a corporate chairperson, the meeting includes reports of profitability and market analysis, announcements of expansion or revision given by the chair, president, or (occasionally) treasurer. Questions and resolutions from shareholders are taken through written submission and from the floor. In addition, the corporate secretary presides over the election of directors and voting on all other resolutions. Annual meetings of shareholders are complicated affairs, carefully rehearsed yet unpredictable. The audience present ususally represents a small fraction of the total number of shareholders. The speech event itself must be studied in tandem with the printed publication of an annual report and proxy statement.

Here is the partial transcript of a question and answer session at an annual meeting of shareholders for a service corporation (DCI). Some questions were submitted in advance; others were submitted in writing at the time of the meeting. All answers were given by the company president.

---

Q:  Why is DCI purchasing its own stock in the market?

A:  We intend to use these shares for our Employee Incentive Plan and we didn't want to dilute the market by issuing new shares. It was recommended to us that, since we have the cash reserves, we purchase the stock in the market, a good suggestion that we've taken.

Q:  Besides the one female director, are there any women in DCI management?

A:  Oh yes. Yes, indeed. There are women in DCI management and the director you refer to is a good example. There are many women in management. Right here at corporate headquarters we have some women in middle management positions.

Q:  Why should this company's top executives receive an average increase of 111% in salary over last year?

A:  Executives' salaries were not increased 111%. The additional compensation you refer to came in the forms of stock options and bonuses in recognition of our banner year of profits.

Q:  What is this company doing to save taxes?

A:  Our treasurer and general counsel keep constant watch on our tax situation. Last year, for instance, we were able to take advantage of the Research and Development Tax Credits, the Investment Tax Credit on equipment, and the Targeted Jobs Program.

Q:  Does DCI plan to expand into new service markets?

A:  We always have expansion plans on the drawing board, expansion both through acquisition and internal start ups. It's our policy, however, never to announce or discuss those plans until they can be operationalized. I believe we have a good record of keeping our shareholders informed of all changes in corporate directions.

---

## DISCUSSION QUESTIONS

1. Describe the speaker's personality (attitudes, predispositions, prejudices, and view-points) from the content, language, and style of his answers. Discuss the speaker's changing credibility as he answers each question.
2. Characterize the relationship between speaker and audience as manifested in the sequence of questions and answers.
3. Speculate on which questions were submitted in advance and which ones came to the speaker without prior reading. On what bases might an audience member calculate the preparedness of a speaker to address a given question?
4. Rank in order from most to least effective the five answers given by this speaker. Discuss a rationale for evaluating the communication effectiveness of such a speaking assignment.
5. If you were a shareholder in DCI and attended the meeting of which this transcript was a part, what impressions of management would be created from this exchange between president and shareholders?

## HYPOTHETICAL SPEECH

Practice the skills of convention planning by designing a one-day conference with at least four different sessions and using at least two of the formats introduced in this chapter. Choose *one* of the following scenarios:

1. You are head of the trust department of a bank, and you invite the twelve trustees of a large union pension fund for an on-site introduction to the bank and its investment practices. Your aim is to convince the trustees, at the end of a one-day meeting, to allow your bank to manage their pension fund.
2. Design a conference to explore the possibilities of a corporation sponsoring major research in conjunction with state universities. In one day, the conference must raise issues of appropriate research, as well as the development and tax contingencies to the corporation in offering such sponsorship. The primary aim of this conference is not persuasion but education.
3. Design a conference to introduce new sales personnel to the product or service lines of your corporation. This convention aims to introduce the field representatives to the products and services as well as to instill in them a sense of corporate identity and pride.

Your assignment is to choose one scenario, fill in the sketch with appropriate details (e.g., names, products, and figures), and design a one-day conference. Develop a printed program with titles, speakers, times, rooms, and session abstracts for the day. The program itself is a sales device to prospective conferees. Be sure that it presents an organized context for the fulfillment of stated aims.

## SUMMARY

A business convention, regardless of purpose, provides a superstructure for public speaking; it constitutes a massive speech event. Convention planning is like speech preparation. Both demand clear objectives, accurate audience analysis, and a sensible structure ensuring communication between speakers and listeners.

Business conventions typically provide three settings for public speech, each requiring different aptitudes and attitudes from a speaker. The general assembly is a large gathering in which speakers and audience members are separated by space, by the trappings of public address (e.g., a sound system and special lighting), and by the expectation of one-way communication. A small group format, by contrast, is less rigid in its physical environment and allows for greater interaction between speaker and audience. The panel format is a kind of group presentation in which each participant contributes a different viewpoint to the exploration of a stated theme or question. These three formats provide unique contexts for the delivery and perception of business speech. A competent speaker and a good listener must take into account the effect of each context on the formulation of meaning.

Planning a business convention, a complex task marked by myriad concerns, follows three basic steps. First, goals must be stated—clear and obtainable objectives must be spelled out. Second, the proper participants must be selected—both the best speakers available to address selected topics and the most appropriate audiences for responding. Third, the logistics of conference management must be attended to—everything from guest accommodations to session facilities.

The most important job of a convention director is the efficient management of time for all participants—speakers and audience alike. Effective scheduling demands consideration of serial order effects (juxtaposition of sessions) and simultaneity (multiple scheduling of the same hour) as well as a recognition of the reasonable limits of audience attention and participation.

Our purpose in discussing the convention setting in a study of business speech is to underscore again the importance of context as a rhetorical variable. While the fundamental principles of public speaking remain constant in all situations, changeable factors such as audience size, physical setup, spatial relationships, and temporal context have impact upon perception and, hence, should influence speech preparation and delivery. The business convention, whether day-long or week-long, imposes constraints and possibilities on the communication process not present in an individual public speech. A student of the art should observe these variables and calculate their effects.

# 12

# Special Consideration: Ghost Writing

Ghost writing involves the composition of a speech by one person and its delivery by another. The ghostly quality derives from an author's invisibility: a ghost written speech is delivered as though it were the sole effort of its speaker. The practice of ghost writing in American business evolves directly from a political model in which campaign speeches are written by a candidate's staff. Equivalents to the corporate ghost writer may also be found in the publication of certain autobiographies identified by the phrase "as told to" or, often, not acknowledging the contribution or name of a ghost writer at all (e.g., the invisibility of ghost writer Alex Haley in *The Autobiography of Malcolm X*). Actually, the title "ghost writer" suggests a too-simple image for a complicated function in the corporate structure. There are many kinds of ghost writers offering different services and requiring various relations with a speaker. Our purposes in this chapter are to discuss the important role of ghost writing in business, to suggest some practical guidelines for its practice, and to raise some ethical questions.

## A GHOST WRITER IN THE CORPORATION

"Speech writer" is a staff position serving the executive echelon in a corporate hierarchy. When asked to speak frequently in public (perhaps twice monthly), many corporate executives lack the time and skill required to meet this demand. Recognizing the importance of such public occasions, most corporations view the salary of a good speech writer as money well spent. Years ago an executive could use the same address with variations for different audiences. With the advent of TV and radio coverage, and with today's increasing press coverage of all corporate communication, a speech cannot be repeated without the audience noticing. Often, advance copies of speeches are requested by journalists, and this makes the speech assignment doubly complicated; it is necessary to create both a verbal and written text. The demand for competent speech writers in business, thus, is increasing. In rare instances, a ghost writer works exclusively for one speaker. More frequently, the speech writer serves a group of executives and may, in some settings, do other kinds of writing or consulting in addition to speech preparation.

In a staff position, the corporate ghost writer works under unusual circumstances. He or she has little if any authority to initiate policy but exercises enormous power in articulating and interpreting policy as presented in public speech. Like any other business communicator, a speech writer may be held accountable by the public for clear communication and by the business institution for accurate representation. These responsibilities for a ghost writer are classified under his or her primary accountability to the speaker.

Public corporate communications depend for their success upon policies and practices consistent across all media and all occasions. A business is identified and judged by the public not only for the quality of its products and services but also for the quality of its communication — its correspondence, reports, speeches, telephone conversations, print and electronic advertising. A corporate image is fashioned by the public communication of many individuals in service, management, and executive positions. Each spokesperson is unique in his or her manner of speech (whether verbal or written), but each must also fit into an integrated circuit of corporate communication. The ghost writer works under the double mandate of representing a corporate viewpoint from the perspective of, and in the voice of, another individual.

## THE WRITER AND THE SPEAKER

Consider the relationship between a public speaker and a ghost writer and the mutual dependence of their experience. There is an intimacy, both exquisite and fearful, in the act of ghost writing. A writer's responsibility to the speaker is akin to the translator's craft or to the playwright's art; yet, neither of these analogies is exact. No apt equivalent exists to a ghost writer's relationship with a speaker.

The writer's role in speech preparation ranges along a continuum from total composition to editorial assistance; an exact job description is determined in each case by the speaker's need and the occasion's demand. One speaker develops a thesis and outline and expects the ghost writer to assist in *research*. In this situation, one must find examples, references, statistics, and other evidence to fill out and support the speaker's argument. In a second kind of relationship, the speaker provides the thesis and all of the supporting materials, while the ghost writer organizes the speech into an *outline*. A third situation calls for a *collaborative* relationship, in which speaker and writer work through the process of composition together from beginning to end. A fourth type of speaker turns over to a writer the complete *creation* of a text and delivers the speech verbatim as supplied. Still another speaker roughs in a speech manuscript and turns to a ghost writer for *editorial* help, a stylistic polishing. These various responsibilities suggest a range of relationships between writer and speaker. Another possibility exists that also deserves mention—the writing of a speech by committee. Whereas many other business tasks can be accomplished best by a group, writing rarely benefits from committee work. Avoid such an assignment.

Whatever the working circumstances of a given speech assignment, the essential talent required of a ghost writer remains constant. He or she must be able to take on the perspective of a speaker and to represent it fully and fairly. A ghost writer's job is *not* to stand apart from a speaker and narrate or comment on a viewpoint. Rather, the job is *to become* the speaker, to embody that viewpoint and to give it a credible voice. This mandate demands deep knowledge of the speaker's philosophy and thought, as well as a practical acquaintance with the speaker's language and delivery. Earlier we suggested that a ghost writer is like a playwright. More accurately, ghost writing calls upon the actor's skill. Writing successfully for another person involves imaginative role playing, an enactment and projection of that person's thinking in that person's manner of speech.

## PROCEDURAL GUIDELINES

The working relationship between a speaker and a writer is molded by organizational circumstances and by the personalities of the individuals involved. Some practical suggestions may help the novice ghost writer to establish an efficient and effective relationship with a speaker. Here are ten guidelines:

1. Develop a simple form for noting a given speech assignment. Ghost writing often occurs under circumstances of great pressure and little time. A simple written agreement between writer and speaker ensures against misunderstandings. Here is a sample:

---

*Speech Writing Assignment Sheet*

Speaker: _____

Writer: _____

Date of speech: _____

Place of speech: _____

Occasion: _____

Subject: ——————————————————————————————

Length (in minutes): ——————————————————————

Due date: ——————————————————————————————

Working title: ————————————————————————————


*Summary of writer's responsibilities* (e.g., research, outline, editorial, complete ms.)

2. Meet with the speaker as early as possible after accepting a speech assignment. Ample lead time in any creative process allows the mind, conscious and unconscious, to get to work and to explore possibilities.

3. Keep a work journal observing precisely a speaker's vocabulary and manner of speech. If you write frequently for the same speaker, notice his or her strengths and weaknesses in delivering humor, telling anecdotes, handling statistics, relating with audiences, and manipulating a manuscript or notes. Write to employ a speaker's strengths and to avoid his or her weaknesses. If an individual's habits of speech or pet vocabulary impede communication success, raise the issue frankly (and confidentially).

4. Write aloud.

5. Type a speech manuscript with triple spacing. Use *italics* or <u>underscoring</u> to encourage emphasis or inflection in delivery. Some speakers prefer a manuscript format with a wide left margin for the headings of an outline. These headings help the speaker to find his or her place quickly if lost.

6. As a general rule, count on a speech delivery of 150 words per minute and calculate the appropriate length in pages accordingly. If graphics or other property aids are used, they slow down the rate of delivery and should be taken into account in meeting a time limit.

7. Keep strictly confidential all meetings and deliberations with a speaker.

8. Whenever possible, meet the speaker for a rehearsal prior to the speech occasion. Performance variables to enhance the speech's impact can be discussed. Also, close revision of the text is best done in rehearsal.

9. Attend the speech or obtain a videotape whenever possible.

10. Conduct a post-speech interview with the speaker to get his or her response to the speech's success.

## SOME ETHICAL QUESTIONS

Any time one person speaks on behalf of another, ethical considerations apply. The invisible authorship of a speech suggests several questions:

Whose opinion and viewpoint, really, are being expressed?
Does the speaker understand fully what he or she is saying and its implications?
Is the audience receiving a fair representation of the speaker's personality and perspective in the content, language, and style of the speech?
Can the writer in good conscience vouch for the truthfulness and fairness of all ideas espoused by the speech?
Can all references in a speech text be verified by the speaker himself or herself?
Have all legal permissions for quoted material been secured?

Ultimately, all ethical and legal considerations of speech authorship come down to one basic question: Can the speaker fully embrace a writer's content and style? Regardless of who did the writing, the speaker is finally accountable for every word and idea that he or she utters. Like the letter or report writer who signs a document actually authored by someone else, it is the signator and speaker who must take full responsibility.

Ghost speech writing is a collaborative effort that, when successful, blends two voices into one and presents a single unified viewpoint. Ghost writing can be a fun and fulfilling challenge. The partnership required between writer and speaker offers one of the finest relationships available in a business enterprise.

## EXERCISES

We have said that a ghost writer's primary obligation is to take on the perspective of a speaker, to become as one with that speaker's voice and viewpoint. Practice the skill by adopting five distinct perspectives toward the same issue. Imagine that a business seminar is being held to address this question: "When a corporate executive makes a decision, to whom is he or she most accountable?"

Now *outline* five responses to the question, taking on the perspectives described below. That is, each perspective (A, B, C, D, E) represents a different speaker for whom you are asked to outline a speech. Structure the best and clearest argument you can design in support of the stated viewpoint.

**A**   When making corporate decisions, an executive is most accountable to *shareholders*.

**B**   When making corporate decisions, an executive is most accountable to *employees*.

**C**  When making corporate decisions, an executive is most accountable to *consumers*.

**D**  When making corporate decisions, an executive is most accountable to the *government* and its regulatory agencies.

**E**  When making corporate decisions, an executive is most accountable to *outside standards* (e.g., a code of morality, concern for the environment, defense of capitalism, democracy, or some other philosophy).

**F**  After writing the five outlines, discuss the following questions:

1. What terms in the seminar's question must be defined to yield a useful debate of the issue?

2. By what metaphor, analogy, model, or other argument could a speaker defend his or her viewpoint without denying the importance of the others?

3. Can you imagine a specific executive decision in which the interests of the constituencies represented by these five positions would be in direct conflict with each other?

4. If asked to address the question yourself, what viewpoint would you espouse?

5. In taking on this ghost writing assignment, can you envision a perspective that you would resist or refuse to adopt?

## SAMPLE SPEECH

Here is the introduction to a one-hour address given by Jon Perry, president of Perry & Associates, to a meeting of the Atlantic Arts Council. As a patron of the arts and as an amateur sculptor himself, Perry was asked to speak on the topic of "Art and Commerce: Strange Bedfellows?" The address was ghost written by a collaborative effort. First, Perry talked through the subject on audio tape. Then, a writer organized and polished the manuscript.

---

My invitation to speak here today on this topic sprang from a request of Margaret Peters back in September that I summarize my experiences as one trained in the fields of accounting and the analysis of financial markets who finds himself stealing at least an hour a day from the office to work in a small sculptor's studio. This request was based, I think, upon a real interest in the relationships between business and art and was based, too, on a certain amusement at the apparent opposition between the two. I confess my own bemusement at this seeming tension.

In giving thought to my remarks today, I've become more convinced than ever before of the distance between art and commerce. I'm convinced, for instance, that a relatively few business executives understand the relationship between aesthetic structure and profitability just as I'm quite certain that many sculptors and painters remain aloof to considerations of commercial appeal in their work. However, the real burden of my talk is not to dwell on the surface disparity between art and commerce but to explain why it is that I think the two approaches to life are compatible.

My belief that art and commerce are, at their best, linked naturally to one another is based partly upon a personal relationship with F.T. Lester, head of a prestigious law firm, who cares as much about 19th-century Russian literature and pre-Columbian art as he does about the charge of discriminatory hiring and promotion practices at this city's First National Bank, for whom Lester is general counsel. It is based upon a life long relationship with Richard Dickinson, retired president of Harcourt Industries, who cares as much about the unique palette of van Gogh as he does about the likelihood of Dow Jones topping 1300. And my conviction that business and art are integrally related is based especially on a view of Shakespeare as the master of both endeavors, as the playwright who protected his own investment in the Globe Theatre by manufacturing first-rate products and who utilized his company's personnel to the utmost by creating characters who gave expression to the special talents of his actors. I believe that this blending of commercial and artistic expertise was the capacity that allowed Shakespeare to live a seven-year's happy retirement away from London and the Globe.

From this introduction alone, we can observe some practical lessons about the ghost writer's craft. Here is a highly personal speech, evidenced by the named reference to Margaret Peters, the personal references to F.T. Lester and Richard Dickinson, and the anecdotal style. The theme of the address draws together its speaker's professional and personal lives. The ghost writer's task, even in these introductory remarks, was to fill out and make tight a loose skeletal framework provided by the speaker. Thus, the Shakespeare example was supplied by the writer as consistent with the speaker's own examples but suggesting greater possibilities for the text's development.

## DISCUSSION QUESTIONS

1. Describe the tone of voice and personality of the speaker as projected in the language and content of this excerpt.
2. From the content and style of this introduction, what expectations are set up in the mind of audience members regarding the speech's further development?
3. Assuming that the speaker is *not* a Shakespeare buff, discuss the ramifications for the speaker, the audience, and the text of the references to Shakespeare provided by the ghost writer.

## HYPOTHETICAL SPEECH

Divide the class into pairs. Each twosome should be given 30 minutes to conduct a two-way interview in response to the question, "Who most influenced your decision to pursue a business career?" Probe each other for a full answer. Secondary questions will need to be asked to explore the why's and how's. Use the full 30 minutes.

Then, without further consultation, ghost write a 3-minute (450 word) speech for the other person, explaining how he or she chose to pursue a business career and the role of one influential person in that decision. Exchange manuscripts and deliver the ghost written speeches.

## SUMMARY

Ghost speech writing is a common practice in American business communication. The writer works in a staff position for one or more corporate executives and is accountable for each assignment to the given speaker. The frequency of public speech invitations, the ubiquity of press coverage, and the necessity of advance copies all encourage executives to rely upon professional help for the composition of speeches.

The relationship between a speaker and a writer makes each dependent upon the other; it demands, thus, a working (and workable) partnership. A ghost writer's specific role in the preparation of a speech varies with circumstances and speakers. Depending upon the assignment, the writer may become a researcher, outliner, collaborator, creator, or editor. Regardless of the actual manuscript responsibility, a ghost writer must try to take on the speaker's perspective, to adopt his or her viewpoint, and to speak with the other's voice. This ability requires an actor's sensitivity and skill.

Some procedural guidelines for managing the relationship between writer and speaker are (1) to record the assignment in writing, (2) to begin the collaboration as early as possible, (3) to keep a journal of the speaker's typical speech behaviors, (4) to write aloud, (5) to type the finished manuscript with triple spacing and appropriate italics or underscoring, (6) to calculate length by a ratio of 150 words per minute, (7) to maintain confidentiality in the relationship, (8) to rehearse delivery with the speaker, (9) to attend the speech whenever possible, and (10) to do a post-speech critique with the speaker.

The working relationship between a ghost writer and a business speaker places certain expectancies on each partner. Ultimately, though, the speaker must be held accountable legally and ethically for every word and idea of the speech as delivered. An effective collaboration can help to ensure the speaker's success and to safeguard the writer's process.

# 13

# Special Consideration:
# The Speech in Print

One special consideration for a business speaker is the possibility of his or her speech getting into print. The public addresses of politicians, statesmen, celebrities, religious leaders, and other figures of prominence are converted to print in newspapers, magazines, pamphlets, and books. Sometimes the speaker controls this dissemination in print, but, in other circumstances, print publication is unanticipated by the speaker and is beyond his or her control. In this chapter, we shall consider the issue of printed speeches by discussing their uses in business, the special characteristics of their extended audience, and some guidelines for the speaker.

## THE USES OF SPEECH IN PRINT

Speech texts become print texts in five ways. First, a business address can be intended for immediate translation into print, seeking its primary audience among readers, not listeners. News conferences and press announcements are in this category of quasi-speech events. In both instances, a company spokesperson addresses reporters with an announcement intended for dissemination to the public. Such messages are launched by speech but published in print, usually newsprint. The intended audience is not the visible assembly of news reporters but the projected circulation of individual readers — an audience invisible to the speaker. Because such speech occasions are intended to find their audience through print, a speaker must make every effort to ensure the accurate transcription of his or her remarks by reporters. A speaker should *read* brief press announcements and, whenever possible, distribute copies to reporters. Also, remember that newspaper writers have word limits and deadlines to meet. Keep press announcements concise with the major points up front in the text's development.

A second way that speech becomes print is as *part* of a news story. Extracts are taken from a speaker's address and used to highlight or support the analysis of a reporter. A speaker has less control over the use of his or her words in this context. Certain parts of a text will be quoted directly, others summarized, and still others deleted. The best one can do to encourage fair reporting of a public address is to deliver a well-organized speech text, clear in its development and easy to follow. In addition, it pays dividends to cooperate with reporters when they seek clarification, or when they ask other questions after a speech. Presumably both speaker and reporter are interested in clear communication, and they need each other to accomplish the task. Business speakers should monitor their press coverage and demand accuracy; at the same time, it is important to avoid an adversary attitude toward reporters.

A third way that a speech makes its way into print is by the official publication of a complete transcript in a newspaper or journal. For example, the major addresses of government officials, as well as special addresses at the United Nations, are published verbatim in the *New York Times* the day after speech delivery. An especially valuable resource for studying current speech transcripts, including business addresses, is the bimonthly journal *Vital Speeches of the Day*, available in most libraries. Often, publication of this kind is arranged in advance and copies of a transcript are supplied to the publisher. On other occasions, the importance of an event or the quality of a speech are unanticipated, and publication is arranged after delivery. In either case, a speech text must be written for its primary audience of listeners but with a view, too, toward a secondary audience of readers. It must *speak* well and *read* well. As we have argued before in this study, human speech is the fundamental metaphor of communication perception, and even silent readers ascribe attributes of voice and performance to a print text.

A fourth way that speech becomes print is in book form, in an anthology of public address. Like the published transcripts of current speeches in a newspaper or journal, an anthology prints the entirety of a speech with an editorial description of the occasion. Book publication represents a major investment of time and money, and only those speeches of lasting value or interest are likely to see print in this form. Before signing permission to publish a speech transcript in a book, a speaker is well advised to reserve rights of revision.

Finally, a business speech may be translated into print by corporate publication. When a top executive has occasion to set forth or summarize an important corporate viewpoint, the publication of that address can have many uses. Usually printed on good paper and bound as a ten- to twenty-page pamphlet, the speech text can become a position paper putting on record a corporate stand for public inspection. Such pamphlets can serve communication objectives with a number of constituencies—employees, shareholders, consumers, and government officials. A professional writer (ghost) is often brought in to edit such texts before publication.

In all of these ways—press announcement, news story, current transcript, inclusion in an anthology, or corporate publication—a business speech takes on a life of its own transcending the occasion of its delivery and the physical presence of its speaker. Print publication can vastly extend the impact of a speech through space and time. A speaker's address, when printed, can reach more readers than any auditorium could hold and can continue to speak days, months, or years after its verbal delivery.

## THE AUDIENCE FOR SPEECH IN PRINT

Audience perception is a vital variable of any communication process. Perceptual differences between reading and listening suggest some special problems for speech in print. Even if the same individuals were to read a speech and attend its delivery, the differences of occasion and medium would elicit some differences in response.

Audience participation in a speech event is a group phenomenon in which response, positive or negative, is shared by all and can be ignited by contagion. A reader's experience, by contrast, is private and grows by incremental rather than geometrical development. The live experience of speech participation is spontaneous, timebound, and unrepeatable. Reading can duplicate these qualities of perception but has an added dimension of reader control. At any time, a reader can speed up, slow down, stop, or repeat the flow of discourse. The possibility for audience deliberation is greater in a reading experience than in a speech setting. Furthermore, environmental variables in the speech and reading experiences can affect different audience perceptions. Generally, such factors as room arrangement, seating, lighting, and volume are in the speaker's control in public address; these situational variables are in the reader's control when the speech reaches print. With all of these differences of perception—group participation versus private reading, spontaneity versus deliberation, speaker control versus reader control— the turf changes, as it were. In moving from speech to print, an audience's power to direct perception increases. Yet, the right to initiate communication remains always with the speaker.

Differences of perception accrue not only from the circumstances of reading and listening; they grow out of differences imposed by the medium of print itself. Print is an orderly medium, even if the thought it contains is not. Sentences and paragraphs come to the reader with an assumption of regularity and symmetry. Print imposes upon discourse a rigid system of visual conformity. Speech, by contrast, can be highly idiosyncratic. Print is uniform, lacking tone or inflection except by the crude suggestions of *italics*, **boldface**, or underscoring. The performance variables of speech allow a much wider and more subtle range of expression to the speaker. Print demands a one-at-a-time focusing process of the reader as he or she moves from left to right across a line and from top to bottom down the page. Speech, on the other hand, is a less structured sense experience permitting the perception of multiple cues simultaneously. Print is an exclusively visual medium;

speech is primarily an aural experience. Print offers little, if any, color variation; speech permits the full spectrum.

These differences of medium do not mean that reading and listening are totally distinct experiences without relation to one another. Obviously, the two are closely linked. The features of environment and voice lacking in a print experience can be supplied by the reader's imagination and, on occasion, these can make startling contributions to a silent reader's perception. Both activities require attention and concentration: good listening and reliable reading are active processes. Both listening and reading involve direct response to the communication initiatives of a speaker (or an implied speaker). Still, the differences remain, and these must be taken into account by the speaker whose address goes into print.

## SOME GUIDELINES FOR SPEECH IN PRINT

The first recommendation for a speaker who anticipates print publication is to include the secondary audience, or readers, as part of one's audience analysis. A speaker's first obligation is to communicate clearly with a live audience, but safeguards can be incorporated into a speech text to serve a secondary audience as well. Readers *perceive* differently; they require a literate speech text akin to a personal essay. Readers also bring to a speech a different *context* than that shared by listeners. Readers may have vested interests in the subject or the speaker entirely unlike the interests of the original listeners. More importantly, readers may approach a speech transcript long after the date of its delivery, and this passage of time alone will alter perception in many ways. Recognizing these contextual variables, a speaker should build into a speech some description of its intended context. The speech's purpose, primary audience, occasion, and date can all be acknowledged in the speech itself and, thus, prescribe limits to its valid interpretation. In addition, the editorial introduction, or abstract, to a printed speech text can extend its useful lifespan by establishing a context for proper reading.

A second recommendation for a speaker who anticipates print publication is to investigate clauses of the copyright law applicable to a given situation. Copyright law is a complicated subject, and its applicability must be studied on a case-by-case basis. As a general rule, any direct quotation must be properly footnoted with a full bibliographical citation and permission must be secured from the copyright holder. Even if quoting material not under copyright (e.g., an unpublished letter or a public lecture), permission to include an extract in a copyrighted publication is required. Whenever questions arise about the "fair use" of copyrighted materials, seek legal counsel or, better, cover all eventualities by securing permission.

A proper footnote citing a quotation from a public speech may follow this format:

Speaker's name, "Title of speech or lecture," Name of sponsoring organization (if applicable), location, date.

Notice that only one period is used in this citation. All internal punctuation uses the comma.

One format for securing permission to quote copyrighted material is the following letter:

---

Dear _____ :


As part of a speech I delivered entitled _____ on _____(date)_____ at
_____(place)_____ , I used the following quotation:




The speech transcript will be published by _____(publisher)_____ on or about
_____(date)_____ . May I please have your permission to include the above quotation? I shall credit your permission by the following line in the published version:




I would appreciate your consent to this request. The right that I seek will in no way restrict other publications of your material in any form. A statement of release is printed below. Please sign, return to me, and keep the attached copy for your files.



Sincerely,


_____

_____(address)_____

---

I (we) grant permission for the use requested above.

_____(date)_____          _____(signature)_____

                              _____(address)_____

A third recommendation for the business speaker who anticipates print publication is a common sense injunction: Do not make any statement in a public speech that you would not want to see in print. As noted in earlier discussion, a speaker cannot always control the use, extent, or dissemination of a speech in print. The best way to guard against misrepresentation or misinterpretation is to exercise caution in the original speech. It is essential to express oneself precisely and with prudence. Be prepared to stand behind any public statement made before any audience, even when the speech reaches readers not present in the original audience. This admonition applies, as well, to private contacts with reporters. "Off the record" is a phrase that has ruined more than one career. Print is a powerful medium, and a careful public figure must be disciplined in his or her speech.

## EXERCISES

**A**   List below ten famous speeches (business or other) that have been preserved for posterity by their print publication. Identify the speech by title, speaker, or quotable line.

_____
_____
_____
_____
_____
_____
_____
_____
_____
_____

**B**    Write a brief essay in which you distinguish the voices appropriate to a business letter, a business report, and the published transcript of a business speech.

**C**   Write a brief essay in which you describe the differences in preparation of a speech to be delivered orally but not published, and one that you know will be printed after delivery. Be specific about changes in the creative process of speech composition resulting from the likelihood of publication in print.

## SAMPLE SPEECHES

Search among the current and back periodical sections of a public or university library for *two* transcripts of business speeches delivered within the past six months. Begin your search in the *New York Times*, the *Wall Street Journal*, and *Vital Speeches of the Day*. Read only complete transcripts, and select two interesting examples that fall within the broad definition of a business speech discussed in Chapter 1 of this book. Fill out the following critique form for each transcript.

*Speech Transcript #1*

Date of speech: _____     Place: _____

Speaker: _____     Affiliation: _____

Title of speech: _____

Occasion: _____

Bibliographical citation of print publication:

Define characteristics of the address that qualify it as a business speech.

What is the speaker's apparent purpose?

Analyze the needs, interests, and attitudes of the speech's original audience.

What differences of perception accrue from reading this speech rather than listening to it? Be specific.

---

*Speech Transcript #2*

Date of speech: _____   Place: _____

Speaker: _____   Affiliation: _____

Title of speech: _____

Occasion: _____

Bibliographical citation of print publication:

Define characteristics of the address that qualify it as a business speech.

What is the speaker's apparent purpose?

Analyze the needs, interests, and attitudes of the speech's original audience.

What differences of perception accrue from reading this speech rather than listening to it? Be specific.

## HYPOTHETICAL SPEECH

Return to any speech you have delivered previously as part of this study. Working from a tape recording or manuscript, prepare a printed pamphlet of the speech transcript. On the cover, include the speech's title, date of original delivery, and your name. At the beginning of the publication, write a one-paragraph description of the speech assignment and context. Be sure to include proper footnotes or endnotes citing all outside references and quotations.

## SUMMARY

A business speaker is responsible foremost for the kind and quality of public communication that takes place in a speech event. When a speech transcript is published, however, the speaker's accountability extends to the medium of print. Business speech texts can reach print in several ways. News conferences and press announcements describe speeches intended primarily for print. Part of a speech may be quoted, summarized, or alluded to in a news story. The entire transcript of an important address may be published in a newspaper or journal immediately after delivery. A speech may be anthologized in book form. Or the public address of an executive may merit corporate publication as a position paper or pamphlet. Whenever a verbal text becomes a print text, words take on a life of their own, apart from the context of their original delivery. Print publication can extend a speaker's voice and viewpoint across space and time.

The reading audience for a speech differs in some important ways from a listening audience, and these differences affect perception. Speech participation is a group phenomenon whereas reading is a private experience. Speech participation is spontaneous, timebound, and unrepeatable whereas reading affords deliberation. Environmental variables are under a speaker's control in a speech event but shift to the reader's control when a speech is published in print. In addition to these differences in circumstance, a reader's perception is altered from that of a listener by the medium of print itself. Print imposes assumptions of order and uniformity on a text originally characterized by the expressiveness and idiosyncracies of a speaker. Reliable cues to the speaker's voice and attitude must be embedded in a speech transcript to cue the proper mental performance of a reader.

Three guidelines for a speaker who anticipates printed publication are (1) to consider the special needs and interests of a secondary reading audience when analyzing the profiles of primary listeners, (2) to investigate applicable copyright laws covering the publishing situation, and (3) to guard against any sloppy, inaccurate, or libelous public statement that might be misconstrued in print.

# 14

# A Philosophical Overview

With this chapter, Part I of our study draws to conclusion. We have learned that the basic principles of business speaking derive from common sense. When one cares deeply enough about a subject and an audience to invest seriously in the communication process, success can be attained. Such investment demands a practical and objective knowledge of the speaker's own viewpoint and corporate perspective, an audience's vested interests and perceptual process, and a text's variables of composition and delivery. Such an investment also demands acknowledgment of a speech's temporal, spatial, and commercial contexts. Effective business speaking involves skills that can be learned not by trick or formula but by concentrated attention to a given act of public communication. In this philosophical overview of the principles of business speech, we shall review the linkage among speaker, audience, and text; comment on the social responsibility of business speakers; and probe the illogic of three common fallacies.

## SPEAKER, AUDIENCE, AND TEXT

Speaker, audience, and text form a conglomerate relationship in any successful speech event. Only by the viable merger of all three are the individual interests of each protected. An uninformed or casual look at public speaking might see the speaker as solely responsible for success, but this is much too simple a view. Real communication is possible only when a speaker and an audience share common ground based on mutual understanding. A well-structured text defines that ground and, like a contract, helps to ensure that understanding.

The speaker's first task is to define a reasonable communication objective within the givens of his or her expertise, the time and space constraints of a speech event, and the needs, interests, and prior knowledge of an audience. It is not enough for a speaker to specify an intention, though without a clear aim all control is lost. Beyond determining an objective (the "what" of speech), a speaker must find some communication strategy to guide an audience's proper perception of that aim. This, then, is the speaker's second task—deciding *how* to present the *what*. The choices available to a speaker in presenting information and affecting persuasion are legion. Many come under the heading of "text," others under the labels of "delivery" or "performance." Because any message must be deemed credible by an audience before it can win serious attention, matters of performance are central to business speech. A speaker's authority to address a given topic before a given audience is manifest in his or her bearing, voice, posture, manner of speech, appearance, and movement—as well as in the content, language, style, and structure of discourse. A third task of the business speaker is to define and acknowledge his or her status as a representative of some larger constituency (e.g., corporation, consumer group, union, or other vested interest). Even the most skilled orator cannot achieve success, however, without the participation of an audience in the communication process.

Audiences for business speech rarely come to a given occasion without corporate and personal biases. The commercial context of business speaking tends to heighten the vested interests of all parties and to eschew neutrality. A listener's private and corporate attitudes toward the speaker and the topic of speech affect perception in substantive ways. The listener's prior knowledge of a subject and status relationship to the speaker also serve as filters of perception. To succeed consistently in speech assignments, one must read an audience, analyzing their predispositions and assessing the depth of the members' commitments. Not only does an audience bring to a speech attitudes likely to affect attention, but the process of perception itself is complex and variable. A smart speaker understands that listeners accumulate meaning over time and that signs of intention are projected both visually and verbally. The study of an audience's role in speech communication benefits both speakers and audiences because theirs is a mutual accountability in the process.

A speech text—*what* is said—gives shape to the shared experience of a speaker and an audience. Textual dimensions include language, style, and structure. A speech text *contains* meaning in an organized form and it *propels* meaning in a sensible direction, guiding both the spatial and temporal perceptions of an audience. An effective text articulates a speaker's intention and facilitates the listener's perception. When words are used precisely, imaginatively, and economically, the language of a text can make the event memorable long after a speech's delivery. In the cases of ghost written speeches and published transcripts, a text takes on substance beyond its author's or speaker's presence. The language and structure of any business speech serves as an implied contract defining and guaranteeing the merger between speaker and audience. A speaker cannot choose words carelessly without offering a flawed or fallacious contract. To construct a text with intelligence and imagination serves both speaker and audience.

## BUSINESS COMMUNICATION AND SOCIAL RESPONSIBILITY

The critical model for speech analysis espoused by this study demands a system of relationships between speaker, audience, and text. As complicated and far-reaching as that system may become for a given speech, any suggestion of closure to the system is mistaken. No business speech is a self-contained event separable from its corporate, commercial, or personal contexts. And no business activity—research, manufacturing, sales, service, or management—can be separated from larger social, political, and cultural contexts. A business speaker has social responsibilities that extend beyond the specific objective of a given speech and that transcend the profit goals of a corporate vision.

This social responsibility comes clearly into focus with the reminder that business speech, regardless of commercial motivation, is an instance of human communication. Ultimately, all public speech prescribes an interpersonal relationship between a speaker and listeners. Good speech encourages an honest and useful relationship, one calculated to serve all parties by explicating facts and clarifying perceptions. Effective speech, like a well-bonded relationship, depends upon a speaker's and a listener's capacities to adopt multiple perspectives toward a given issue. A speaker models this attitude by acknowledging a listener's perspective while presenting forcefully the values of one's own viewpoint.

In working out an ideal of competent business speech, one encounters myriad ethical dilemmas. Short-term profits can conflict with long-term gains. The credibility of a speaker, like that of a product name, depends finally upon consistent performance. A good speaker protects ethical integrity by presenting facts before interpretation, by grounding persuasive appeals in ample information, and by protecting the free choice of respondents. A good speaker, thus, will not coerce or manipulate change in an audience by means of flattery, bullying, exaggeration, withholding information, or other deceit. By avoiding these fallacious appeals, a speaker reserves the privilege of reasoned argument to present and substantiate a viewpoint.

In addition to a business speaker's interpersonal and ethical responsibilities, he or she must also be held accountable for the evolution of a language. All public communicators are special trustees of the language. The use of jargon and clichés by business speakers drains vitality from the common inheritance of all users of that language. Business communicators, as much as professional writers and orators, must exercise precision and imagination in their use of language if the common ground of understanding is not to erode. By serving language, a speaker serves all business constituencies and preserves cultural (and commercial) profits.

## THREE FALLACIES

When discussing the relationships among speaker, audience, and text, we have probed beneath the surface of public address to analyze underlying principles. These discussions, while philosophical in nature, have been pragmatic in intent. Our aims from the beginning have been to improve the quality of business oratory and the reliability of audience perception. We may hope that our view of business speech is not so simple or narrow as it was at the beginning of this study. Our critical framework for evaluating speech success has demanded rather careful, rather sophisticated analysis. The purpose of this mental effort has not been to obfuscate the subject but to enlighten the student—to increase practical understanding.

Still, business speaking remains an apparently simple term that evokes familiar images. Despite thorough study and careful practice, fallacious connotations surrounding the term may continue to impede progress. Three fallacies are particularly intractable.

### "The end justifies the means."

This hackneyed statement describes a popular fallacy from the point of view of many business speakers. Under its auspices are justified a variety of hard-sell techniques so concentrated upon audience response as to ignore completely the means of attaining that response. When a speaker ignores any aspect of the communication *process* (the means) and focuses solely on the sale of a product or idea (end), all regard for the listener's rights and perceptions is eliminated. The fallacy of this approach is that it leaves no room for a genuine relationship between speaker and audience in a speech text. Yet, experience teaches that real speech communication depends entirely on such a relationship. All of a speaker's rhetorical choices and all of a listener's critical responses seek to establish meaningful contact between participants. A philosophy of public address that ignores the means of forming and maintaining that relationship is doomed to failure, despite the misguided enthusiasm of adherents. Interestingly, such a fallacious approach to speech communication also undermines long-term commercial profits.

### "Business speakers are puppets of a corporate voice."

The second fallacy shifts attention from the speaker to the audience. The judgment that a speaker is a mere pawn of corporate interests comes from a listener's perspective. The allure of this viewpoint is its *partial* truth: a business speaker does represent a constituency larger than himself or herself, and one does not speak in a commercial context simply as a private citizen. The fallacy of this statement centers on an exaggerated perception of corporate control over individual speakers. Ultimately, every speaker, regardless of the context, must be held personally and legally accountable for the accuracy and validity of a speech as delivered. The extent to which an individual speech reflects or does not reflect a corporate viewpoint does not change the degree of individual accountability of a speaker for what is said.

### "Business speeches are invariably dull affairs."

This third fallacy shifts perspective again from a speech audience to the text itself. There is no denying that many business speeches are dull affairs, burdened by illogic, expressed in ill-conceived language, and (occasionally) delivered with ill will. The fallacy of this statement resides in the adverb "invariably." Dullness is *not* an inevitable hallmark of business speech. When a text is dull, the blame can be fixed only in one place—a speaker's incompetence. Well-written and skillfully delivered business speeches can be insightful, imaginative, timely, persuasive, and exciting events. Indeed, if the assignment is appropriate to an audience and an occasion, and if a speaker has prepared well, the business speech *should* exhibit these rhetorical virtues.

## SUMMATION

The business speech is a theatrical event set on a workaday stage. Its public address is directed at every turn by a speaker, but the quality of its dramatic engagement depends equally upon the responsiveness of an audience. This mutual performance played out by speaker and listener is cued by the structure and language of a speech text. Like a well-made play, the text of a business speech guides the audience from exposition through complications to a crisis of decision and on to a climax of response. At each turning point of organization, the speech text brings into close relation a speaker's intention and a listener's perception.

The composition, delivery, and reception of any business speech form an integrated circuit, a system of communication. This system, in turn, derives meaning from broader contexts of commercial, corporate, political, and social realities. These contextual variables take on tangible presence in a speech event by the sure sense of representation between speaker and audience. All participants in a business speech event are defined in part by their implicit or explicit constituencies (e.g., corporate executives, shareholders, employees, consumers, customers, suppliers, competitors, members of the financial community, or agents of government or industry regulation). To understand fully the dynamics of a given business speech and its effect upon an audience, these vested interests and constituency perspectives must be taken into account. The manifest and subtle tensions arising from these conflicting viewpoints form the backdrop of speech perception and can charge an apparently mundane occasion with extraordinary energy.

Business speaking is practiced in every division of corporate activity, on all levels of a hierarchy, and by all interested parties inside and outside the corporate frame. By means of public address and debate, business policies are formulated and promulgated, products are introduced and sold, consumer rights are defended, corporate profits are enhanced, and community health and welfare are protected. Only when the quality of business speech is of the highest caliber will these various interests be properly served. Such excellence demands deliberate study and practice from business speakers and close attention and reasonable response from business audiences. When a speech text can ensure the close engagement of speaker and listener from beginning to end, all participants will be enriched in the drama of human communication.

This chapter concludes the major portion of our study. What follows are brief discussions and samples of eight common types of business speeches.

# II

# THE PRACTICE OF
# BUSINESS SPEAKING

Each of the brief chapters to follow considers a specific kind of business speech. While the range of possible topics and strategies for speaking is almost limitless, the samples contained here form a core of conventional assignments that are repeated often in most business settings.

The linkage between theory and practice (between Parts I and II of our study) forms a pragmatic and fluid relationship. The suggested formats and sample speeches included in these chapters are just that, "suggestions" and "samples." They are illustrative, not prescriptive.

Each chapter follows an eight-part outline beginning with a "definition" of the speech type. Then, separate consideration is given to the roles of "speaker," "audience," and "text" in the communication system of that speech. A "suggested format" offers a generic outline, and a "sample speech" illustrates the type. A "hypothetical speech" invites you to have a go at a specified assignment. Finally, a "critique form" is included for evaluating student or professional speech samples.

# 15

# Speech of Introduction

## DEFINITION

A speech of introduction points audience attention to an event beyond itself. Whether introducing another speaker, a film, or some other instance of public communication, the introductory speech serves three essential functions. First, it provides information necessary for the audience to fully appreciate or understand what is to come. This information most often concerns a speaker—his or her professional credentials and special qualifications. This expository information also may focus upon the subject to be addressed in the main event. The second function of an introductory speech, beyond exposition, is to prepare the audience for their listening role. Thus, a good introduction gains the audience's attention, encourages a positive audience attitude toward the event to come, and provides a springboard for the next speaker's presentation. A third function of the introductory speech is to facilitate the main speaker's work—to make him or her feel welcome and to establish an atmosphere in which that speaker will feel at ease.

## SPEAKER

When assigned to give a speech of introduction, one must assess the total context in which the presentation will be made. Specifically, one must find out the purpose of an entire speech event and decide, thus, how to further that purpose with a good introduction. As with any other speech assignment, one must analyze an audience's interests, needs, and prior knowledge to select the right information and to choose an appropriate style. One must learn the intended length of a speech event to calculate a proper length for the introduction.

A speaker's most important task when giving an introduction is to become thoroughly familiar with the person, persons, or thing to be introduced. One cannot serve any of the three functions outlined above unless one *knows* well the subject of introduction. For this reason, a close associate is often asked to introduce the speaker. When assigned to introduce a stranger, the speaker should request a current resumé and glean from it the information most relevant to the occasion. Whenever possible, one should arrange to meet the main speaker (or, say, to preview a film) and to gather information not available on a resumé.

Proper delivery of an introduction varies according to occasion. Two guidelines may be helpful in practicing delivery. First, the introduction should match in performance expectations the same level of formality or informality demanded by the main speech event. Second, the introduction should be delivered in a manner calculated to put the audience and the main speaker at their ease. Avoid any choice of composition or delivery likely to cause or to increase tensions. A good introduction reduces, not increases, barriers to communication.

## AUDIENCE

A listener's demands of an introduction are few but important. An introductory speech must explain *what* is to come and must give evidence by its manner or content *why* the main event is important. Speech audiences typically come to an occasion positively predisposed: a good introduction encourages that attitude. Listeners also expect of a good introduction clarity and brevity. The latter virtue is an essential key to success with this type of speech.

## TEXT

The text of an introductory speech can take one of several forms. In formal settings, an introduction begins with an acknowledgment of the audience and names any dignitaries present in decreasing order of organizational rank. For example, "Mr. President, members of the board of directors, and fellow employees." A formal introduction proceeds to list the academic and professional credentials of a speaker. Less formal introductions do not recognize distinctions among audience members, may be anecdotal in structure, and often use humor. A warning should be given, however, regarding humor. Unless a speaker is an expert joke teller (and unless the joke is specifically relevant to the situation), an attempt at humor can backfire.

Generally, the shorter an introduction is, the better. For a fifteen-minute main speech, an introduction should not exceed two minutes. For a ten-minute main speech, the introduction can be accomplished in one minute. An introduction that runs too long may have serious consequences on audience attitude and attention.

A good text of introduction draws attention away from the present speaker and points toward the main event. Introductions are, by definition, occasions of modesty. Every word, image, idea, and anecdote in an introduction has the aim of bonding a speech audience to the speaker being introduced, *not* to the introducer.

## SUGGESTED FORMATS

Here are two suggested formats for a speech of introduction; one is for formal occasions and the second is for informal situations. Many other outlines are possible.

### Suggested Format 1: Formal Introduction

1. Address to audience with acknowledgment of dignitaries.
2. Recital of speaker's credentials by category (e.g., academic, professional, service) or by chronology (i.e., a timeline of achievement).
3. Statement of speech topic.
4. Welcome to speaker.

### Suggested Format 2: Informal Introduction

1. Welcome to audience.
2. Anecdotal introduction (e.g., story of personal experience with the speaker, comic tale or joke appropriate to speaker or occasion).
3. Summary of speaker's qualifications.
4. Presentation of speaker.

## SAMPLE SPEECH

At a national convention of American business executives addressing issues of the federal tax structure, Arthur Peterson was the keynote speaker. He gave a speech of 35 minutes before a full auditorium of over 1200 conferees, plus a large press corps. Introducing the keynote speaker was Catherine Rinehart. Following is the text of the introductory speech.

---

On April 15, 1982, Arthur Peterson published an open letter to the United States Congress and to the President of the United States regarding the philosophy of federal taxation. In that letter, Mr. Peterson wrote, "Our system of taxation rewards borrowing and penalizes saving. Our system of taxation has mortgaged America's future rather than investing in it."

These statements are strongly worded and radically at odds with current governmental policy; yet, they reflect common sense, not revolutionary thought. They have had impact in governmental circles, coverage from the media, and interest among intellectuals. Our invitation to Mr. Peterson to address this body today is in response to his serious case for a new philosophy of federal taxation.

You know the biography of Arthur Peterson well. He has served on the economic advisory council of three administrations—two Republican and one Democrat. He has escaped the charge of partisanship in all of his public service spanning twenty years in and out of government. As a thinker and writer, publishing twelve books and writing scores of articles, he has forced the attention of scholars and economic theorists to the practical and current circumstances of American politics and economic policy.

Arthur Peterson's views have been read alternately as friendly and unfriendly toward American business interests but never as adversary to the American businessperson. As an economic policy maker and theorist for more than twenty years, he is uncommonly qualified to address current problems with insight. We are here to listen and, over the days to come, to debate. Never before has the American system of taxation and corresponding government spending been so widely questioned and so unquestionably in need of revision. Here is a man of vision.

Ladies and gentlemen, Mr. Arthur Peterson.

---

## HYPOTHETICAL SPEECH

*Write* a one-minute speech introducing a faculty member in your college, university, or professional seminar. The text, no more than 150 words in length, should summarize the instructor's most salient credentials for addressing the subject of his or her specialization.

Research for this short introduction may require an interview and will necessitate reading a resumé.

## CRITIQUE FORM

Find an opportunity to observe an introduction to a public speech. Evaluate the introducer's effectiveness by completing the following form:

*Speech of Introduction*

Critic: _____

Date of speech: _____   Place: _____

Occasion: _____   Speaker: _____

Introducer: _____

1. Summarize the event's context (i.e., speech objective, audience profile, and environmental variables):

2. Outline the introduction and characterize its style:

3. Time of delivery in minutes: _____

4. Evaluate the communication merits and demerits of this introduction for the occasion:

# 16

# Acceptance Speech

## DEFINITION

A speech of acceptance is made in response to an award or a recognition of achievement given to a speaker. Acceptance speeches are often highly personal and rightly so. The presentation of an award acknowledges individual excellence and expects an individual response. But the ceremonial context of an acceptance speech infuses the event with a public significance that transcends personal interests. The existence and title of an award, the selection of a presenter, and the occasion on which an award is given all define a social or institutional context. Accepting an award symbolizes acceptance of the context, too — the identity and aims of an organization. To accept an award is to express solidarity with the values and goals of the group presenting that award. An acceptance speech, thus, is an act of personal communication as well as a symbol of cultural values.

## SPEAKER

The speaker is both subject and object for an acceptance speech, and whenever talking about oneself in public, certain cautions are advised. The presentation of an award elicits pride but ought not to provoke shortsightedness. A good speech of acceptance sets personal achievement in a proper context. It acknowledges a speaker's debts to others and offers thanks for the unusual pleasure of public recognition. Neither boastfulness nor false modesty are appropriate to an acceptance speech. Humility, courtesy, (and brevity) are hallmarks to attain.

When a speaker knows in advance that an award will be given, one has time to reflect on the achievement and to accept with appropriate remarks. With lead time, however, one should not distill out of a speech all emotion and spontaneity. The speech should project an individual's feelings and thoughts on the occasion. When an award is presented as a surprise to the speaker, no advance preparation is possible. In such circumstances, two good rules are to collect one's thoughts before speaking (the audience will wait) and to keep the remarks short.

As noted in the definition, an acceptance speech is part of a larger social and cultural system. To be absent for one's own award presentation may be viewed by the audience as a breach of etiquette or, worse, as a rejection of the group. Whenever possible, thus, a speaker should attend an awards presentation and take seriously the opportunity of an acceptance speech. On occasion, one is called upon to accept an award on behalf of another person or as a representative of a group. In both cases, the thrust of an acceptance speech should direct attention away from the proxy and to the absent recipient.

## AUDIENCE

The audience for an acceptance speech is usually comprised of individuals who share the group values represented by an award and who may have voted to select the recipient. As a result, the audience at an awards banquet, honors convocation, or other ceremony of recognition bring to the event high spirits of solidarity and celebration. They expect the recipient of an award to be pleased, grateful, and reflective. They expect a recipient to take the award seriously and, thereby, affirm the group's importance. It is not hard to please an audience on such occasions if a speaker exhibits the hallmarks of speech excellence described above. However, it is possible to displease an audience by violating their expectations. If an award recipient is absent without sufficient reason, flippant, boastful, argumentative or ungrateful, an awards audience can feel that group integrity has been challenged. An audience can ostracize a speaker sometimes for years to come for inappropriate speech behavior when accepting an award. This is, admittedly, an extreme case. The more usual relationship between speaker and audience at an awards ceremony is one of affection, joy, and celebration.

## TEXT

The words spoken in acceptance of an award must project a speaker's personality and protect a group's integrity. They should express what one thinks *and* how one feels. Typically, an acceptance speech is composed of three parts. First, a speaker thanks the group presenting the award and acknowledges its significance as a symbol of the group's values. Second, one expresses honestly and forthrightly whatever one feels in response to the personal recognition. Third, when appropriate, one acknowledges the unnamed support group whose work and achievement is also represented in the award.

A gracious, sincere, and thoughtful speech of acceptance is itself a personal achievement that justifies in the minds of an audience a recipient's deserving qualifications. Unless a formal acceptance speech is expected for a special award, most recipients are well advised to keep their acceptance speeches to the point and brief.

## SUGGESTED FORMAT

1. Acknowledgment of the award and statement of gratitude to the presenter (or voters or selection committee).
2. Personal statement of appreciation and reflection upon the achievement represented by the award.
3. Recognition of unnamed contributors to the achievement represented by the award.
4. Reiteration of thanks and a show of solidarity with the group's identity and values.

## SAMPLE SPEECH

Here is an acceptance speech delivered by Rhoda Martin when presented with the "Outstanding Young Teacher" award by the Industrial Training Council.

It's an especially great honor to be named an "outstanding young teacher" by the Industrial Training Council—an organization devoted to instructional excellence. "Outstanding" is a compliment usually reserved for mature teachers whose excellence has been shaped by experience over many years. Teaching is an art that requires a long apprenticeship, and I'm still serving mine. I'm trying to acquire the high skills necessary to ensure real learning in a classroom and measurable growth in students.

Any competence that I have developed as a young teacher is the direct result of sitting in the classrooms of truly outstanding teachers and learning something of their ways and attitudes. Especially I acknowledge with gratitude the models of Hiram Park and Pierce Franklin, whose caring attitude toward students and whose professional expertise set the highest standards. I continue to grow as a teacher by rubbing shoulders everyday at PMI with others on our training staff. With them, I share this recognition. Again, thanks to the Industrial Training Council for this high award.

## HYPOTHETICAL SPEECH

Imagine that you have been presented an award as a promising young manager. Write a one-minute acceptance speech.

## CRITIQUE FORM

Find an opportunity to observe an acceptance speech. Evaluate the award recipient's effectiveness by completing the following form:

---

*Acceptance Speech*

Critic: _____

Date of speech: _____     Place: _____

Occasion: _____     Speaker: _____

Award: _____

1. Summarize the event's context (i.e., audience profile, environmental variables):




2. Outline the acceptance speech and characterize its style:



---

3. Time of delivery in minutes: _____

4. Evaluate the communication merits and demerits of this acceptance speech for this occasion:

# 17

# After Dinner Speech

## DEFINITION

An after dinner speech is unique in the repertoire of common business addresses. Its primary purpose is not to inform or to persuade; its first aim is to entertain. This type of speech gets its name from the banquet setting in which a master of ceremonies directs an evening's dinner entertainment climaxed by an entertaining, usually witty, address by a special speaker. The term has expanded its application to contexts other than the banquet circuit and carries now a generic connotation of any public speech offered in a casual or formal setting among colleagues for the purpose of entertainment. An after dinner speech may take various forms and fill different lengths of time, but its aim remains the same. That an after dinner speech may also inform or move an audience are added virtues of a good text.

## SPEAKER

Effective delivery of an after dinner speech requires as much or more preparation than does a heavy policy pronouncement or a sales pitch. On other, more serious occasions, a speaker may rely on the importance of a message or of the event itself to ensure audience attention. In an after dinner speech, the speaker himself or herself must command and retain audience attention. Most entertainers agree that comedy is the hardest performance mode to achieve, and genuine laughter is the most difficult audience response to evoke.

An after dinner speaker must rehearse to achieve the appearance of spontaneity and control. The casual setting of a banquet or other occasion suggests an open, informal relationship between speaker and audience. This means that notes or manuscript must be used sparingly. The manner of delivery should express a speaker's conviviality. The performance of humor (especially joke- or story-telling) depends upon the quality of textual material *and* upon the timing of delivery. While the occasion of an after dinner speech often finds the audience in a festive mood, the speaker must be in complete control of himself or herself and of the speech text. (Avoid overeating or immoderate drinking before an after dinner speech.)

An invitation to deliver this kind of speech carries with it an expectation of the speaker's competence to do the job well. It is a bad mistake to accept the assignment and then try to emulate the style of some celebrity entertainer. A speaker should be himself or herself and let the occasion dictate an appropriate subject and approach.

## AUDIENCE

Audience members for an after dinner speech are usually well sated and primed for an entertaining address. Unlike the pressurized contexts of most business speech, the banquet setting encourages fellowship and good humor. There is less time consciousness than in other settings, and vested interests with their implied conflicts are minimized. An audience for this kind of speech expects to respond with laughter and is willing to take a comic view of themselves and of the usually serious subjects of a business context.

The environmental variables of an after dinner speech affect audience perception. Sitting around tables in haphazard arrangements, accompanied by friends as well as colleagues, and with a beverage nearby, audience members often move about, exchange glances, or even talk to each other during the speech. A good speaker learns to appreciate and to work with these variables, orchestrating them to good effect.

## TEXT

The possible subjects and styles of after dinner speeches vary as widely as individual imaginations. One type may be structured as a sequence of jokes, another as a short anecdote or long story. One may be tongue-in-cheek, another straightforward. One may be highly sophisticated, another down-home. Whatever the approach, the text for an after dinner speech should avoid confrontation (including sarcasm) with an audience.

Three guidelines may be helpful in selecting material and determining delivery for an after dinner speech:

1. Decide an appropriate length for the speech, and choose a topic that can be handled within that limitation. Remember that it is better to send an audience home wishing that the speech had been longer than regretting it wasn't shorter.
2. Choose a subject that will interest an audience by its relevance to their lives and by its freshness or newness. This criterion may be satisfied by addressing a familiar subject from a new perspective.
3. Find a comfortable manner of delivery that fits the speaker's personality and reflects the tone of the occasion as a whole.

## SUGGESTED FORMATS

So many structures are available for an after dinner speech that a single generic outline is not useful. In addition to the earlier suggestions (sequence of jokes and series of anecdotes), here are two typical approaches:

### Suggested Format 1: Biography

For a speech honoring an award recipient or other special guest, a biographical structure is appropriate. Biographical speeches may be organized in reverse chronology starting with a subject's present achievements and working back through time, or in a sequence beginning with early accomplishments and proceeding through time to the present. A third method of organizing biographical material is by category (e.g., academic degrees, design or manufacturing achievements, leadership experience). A biographical speech in the after dinner setting works best not as a verbal resumé but as a personal (and personalized) history.

### Suggested Format 2: Analogy

A speech organized by analogy begins by setting out the terms of comparison between two objects, processes, or persons. The comparative analysis, then, proceeds by defining a sequence of shared qualities, always identifying first the more familiar component and second the object, process, or person of focus.

## SAMPLE SPEECH

Here is an after dinner speech developed by a structure combining biography and analogy. The speech honors the 50th wedding anniversary of a corporate chairman at a banquet in the couple's honor. The speaker compares the success of a marriage to success in business and, thereby, infuses an amusing presentation with personal substance. The audience for this speech was comprised of management-level employees and their spouses. The speaker was a second vice-president.

It is my pleasure to participate in this special day honoring James's and Francine's 50th wedding anniversary. Mine is a double pleasure: to honor the Kennedys and to represent, as well, an honorable group, to which I am proud to belong, the generation of managers and executives who got their start at Winthrop Industries under the tutelage of James Kennedy. We view ourselves as "long-term investments"—an apt description because we are, in a real sense, the living and visible portfolio of the Kennedys' personal investments, the inevitable signs of progress or regress in the corporate vision.

It is a great accomplishment for any small corporation simply to survive five decades in the black. That the incorporation of James and Francine has not merely survived that span of years but continues to grow and prosper, with the value of its stock rising steadily, is an extraordinary accomplishment.

The factors that have contributed to the success of the James-Francine union are the same ingredients that must go into any long-range corporate plan, if the endeavor is to succeed. First, the union represents the merger of two strong individuals. Each one brought to the new corporation a unique and rich heritage. But a successful corporation is not only based upon the merger of independently strong components. It must be based, too, upon a flexible vision, adaptable to the times, and ready to diversify, as the company's talents and resources grow.

A large portion of the James-Francine success must be attributed to their capacity for, and willingness to diversify interests and resources. Over fifty years, they have invested themselves in such far-ranging endeavors as family, industry, civic and church activities, finance, travel, art, and sport. Along the way, they have sunk roots in three cultures—the U.S., Canada, and Mexico.

So the success that we celebrate today is an accomplishment based upon the individual strengths of James and Francine and upon their corporate strength. Tonight we shall present you with several tokens of our esteem. But, in the final analysis, there is only one tribute that an investment can make to its investors, and that is to return a profit. And so, James and Francine, it is our hope for your 50th anniversary that we, in whom you've invested so much, are in some measurable way paying off.

## HYPOTHETICAL SPEECH

Write a 15-minute after dinner speech in which you profile the biography of a renowned personality, living or dead. You may approach the assignment as a serious memorial or as a comic roast.

## CRITIQUE FORM

Find an opportunity to observe an after dinner speech. Evaluate the award recipient's effectiveness by completing the following form:

---

*After Dinner Speech*

Critic: _____

Date of speech: _____     Place: _____

Occasion: _____     Speaker: _____

Subject: _____

1. Summarize the event's context (i.e., audience profile, environmental variables):

2. Outline the after dinner speech and characterize its style:

---

3. Time of delivery in minutes: _____

4. Evaluate the communication merits and demerits of this after dinner speech for this occasion:

# 18

# Sales Speech

## DEFINITION

The term "sales speech" suggests some of the most popularly held images of business communication. Yet, many more product and service sales can be attributed to media advertising, direct mail, and interpersonal contacts than to public speech. A sales address has the avowed aim of persuading consumers to purchase a product, a service, or a proposal. Occasionally, the speaker alone is expected to make a sale. More frequently, however, public address is one component in a larger sales strategy that includes print material and personal contacts.

A sales speech may be delivered in the convention format and, as such, becomes one of a series of persuasive appeals directed to an audience. Each successive speech serves as an exhibit in language of the item to be sold. Under other circumstances, a sales presentation may be the only event in the speech setting. Sometimes the sales event is organized and directed by the seller and, other times, by the buyer. Whatever the circumstances, a sales speech has a clear end goal, and its success can be measured by specific audience response (e.g., purchase, negotiation, or adoption).

## SPEAKER

When delivering a sales speech, one is under special obligation to know thoroughly the product, service, or proposal being sold. The speaker is a spokesperson for that item and for all those involved in its manufacture or creation. One becomes the corporate insignia, as it were, representing and defending the best of its production. A good salesperson should be able to answer all questions regarding design, manufacture, price, delivery, warranty, and repair of a product. What is more important, a good speaker who has analyzed well an audience's needs can anticipate the areas of greatest interest and concern and can construct a speech accordingly. Often, with a sales speech, opportunity for questions and answers is provided. Here, as much as in the speech itself, a salesperson can show his or her product knowledge. The reputation of a product, service, or proposal rests on the speaker's credibility.

When selling, a speaker must understand that he or she represents more than the thing itself. In a very real sense, the speaker must first sell himself or herself to the audience. One's enthusiasm for the product or service can be contagious in the openness and responsiveness of a listener. To achieve this affirmative relationship, however, a speaker's product confidence must be *apparent*; it must be visible and audible on every dimension of speech performance.

## AUDIENCE

Audience perception of a product, service, or proposal is linked inextricably to their perceptions of the speaker and of the corporation represented. All of the design features highlighted in a product (e.g., styling, efficiency, reliability, and precision) should display their counterparts in a speaker's presence. No audience will believe that a product is well designed if its sales proposal is not; no audience will have confidence in a product's strength if its sales presentation is based on weak logic or insufficient evidence.

Two kinds of audiences attend business sales speeches. The first is comprised of consumers who may actually buy and use the product or service. This audience must be assured of the product's quality and dependability; its members are interested primarily in usefulness and economy. A second audience is comprised of distributors—wholesalers, retailers, and franchise owners. These listeners are also interested in product dependability and economy. In addition, distributors want to know all about pricing, discounts, storage requirements, delivery time, return policy, warranty, advertising, and the manufacturer's market analysis. The same sales speech will not serve both audiences equally well.

When listening to a sales presentation—whether in the office, on the phone, or in a public forum—one is rightly skeptical of product claims. One wants and deserves evidence, some guarantee of the speaker's promises. This audience caution is a natural variable of the sales speech. Rather than responding defensively to a listener's questions and concerns, a speaker should appreciate and work with that caution. It is the speaker's responsibility to explain and defend advantages of a given product or service.

## TEXT

The three most common rhetorical patterns used to construct a sales speech are (1) list of reasons, (2) comparative advantages, and (3) criteria satisfaction. With the "list of reasons" approach, one assumes that an audience has a prior interest in the product or service and is favorably predisposed. What they now require to make a purchase, a commitment, are some rational reasons supporting the decision. Always state reasons in a sequence of decreasing importance, from most to least compelling. With the "comparative advantages" approach, one assumes that an audience has already decided to purchase a product or service but has not decided yet which brand or manufacturer to choose. By illustrating the comparative design, efficiency, or cost benefits of one's own product versus the qualities of competing brands, a speaker addresses the buyer's concerns. With the "criteria satisfaction" approach, a speaker offers professionally accepted standards for judging product excellence and shows how his or her product meets those standards. Such a persuasive strategy assumes that a speaker has the professional expertise to know such standards, that such standards indeed exist and can be measured, that they are agreed upon by others, and that the audience would be otherwise unaware of such standards. The choice of which rhetorical structure to use depends, then, upon the nature of a product or service, the expertise of a speaker, and the needs or predispositions of an audience. The last is particularly important because an approach suited to one set of audience needs may be entirely inappropriate to other listeners.

Occasionally, an audience may be persuaded to purchase on the spot because of a sales speech. More frequently, the speech is expected to contribute to a decision-making process that reaches its end at a later time. For this reason, a good sales text must be memorable. Its logical development and rhetorical validity must be compelling at the moment of presentation and must retain appeal beyond the speaker's own presence. Delivery must underscore key words and concepts. Whenever possible, graphics, props, or printed handouts should be used to link aural memory with visual support.

## SUGGESTED FORMATS

### Suggested Format 1: List of Reasons

1. Introduce the product, service, or proposal.
2. List in order of decreasing importance the reasons why someone should purchase. Link each reason to an audience need. Include such considerations as design, efficiency, materials, cost, warranty, and corporate reputation.
3. Summarize the product's virtues and reiterate the most compelling reason to purchase.
4. Call for a purchase response.

## Suggested Format 2: Comparative Advantages

1. Introduce the product, service, or proposal, and explain its features.
2. Introduce the major competitors.
3. Present a feature-by-feature comparative analysis pointing up the advantages of one's product over the competition.
4. When possible, illustrate the comparative data with a summary chart or table.
5. Summarize product virtues and call for a purchase response.

## Suggested Format 3: Criteria Satisfaction

1. Introduce the "class" of products to which one's specific product, service, or proposal belongs.
2. Delineate the accepted criteria for judging excellence in this class of products.
3. Illustrate how one's product satisfies each criterion.
4. Explicate the logical conclusion that one's product excells by satisfying all criteria.
5. Call for a purchase response.

## SAMPLE SPEECH

Jack James is Coordinator of Media Services for a computer firm. He specializes in serving the computer needs of professionals in radio, TV, film, and the print media. On the occasion of this speech, Mr. James has been invited to make a short presentation at the National Conference of Booksellers — Textbook Division. The audience is comprised of textbook editors and sales managers from over fifty large publishing firms. The aim of this speech is to arouse interest among the listeners in a new approach to textbook selling and to suggest the positive contribution of computers to this process. His immediate aim, thus, is to sell a proposal and, thereafter, to sell computers.

Thank you for permitting me five minutes on your busy schedule to propose a time-saving, profit-making plan for textbook sales. It's a subject that I know from both sides. As a former sales manager for a textbook publisher, I'm keenly aware of the critical timing involved in selling to the textbook market. As an occasional university instructor of marketing, I can feel the pressure of order deadlines. From both sides, I know that the volume of sales can depend entirely on getting examination copies out in time for instructor evaluation. An examination copy that arrives one week or even one day after the order deadline is a loss, not a profit.

As you know, the usual approach to textbook sales is to direct mail advertising brochures with tear-offs for examination copies. These are processed at corporate headquarters, coordinated with local representatives, and sent out from a distribution center. The usual turnaround time from the day that a professor puts the card in the mail until he or she receives a book is five to six weeks. That time can be accelerated to a three- to four-week turnaround if the examination copy is requested through the rep rather than mail response. In either case, the time elapsed between initial interest and payoff is directly related to sales. The longer the time is between an expressed interest in the book and a book in the hand, the less likely a sale is to be made. Studies conducted independently by Cooper and A.B. Franklin and reported in *National Textbook Review* indicate a direct correlation between time elapsed and sales probability.

From personal experience, I can vouch for the logic of these results. When six weeks elapse between a mail order and a delivery, an instructor often forgets that he or she even had an interest in adopting the book. The order of an examination copy was a no-risk impulse easily forgotten. IF, however, that book could arrive in a professor's hands within days (not weeks) of ordering it, textbook sales would be increased dramatically.

Two large firms represented here today have already put in place a simple method for accelerating turnaround time, and it will not be long before all others will need to adopt similar systems to compete.

By computerizing requests for examination copies, an order can be processed on the spot of the request and mailed from the distribution center the same or the next day. At relatively little cost, local representatives can be outfitted with a simple terminal tied directly to the distribution center. The rep enters the request, verifies his or her identity, and, essentially, processes his or her own order. When a professor expresses an interest in a certain book, the representative can make the order that day, and the book can be in the mail the next.

In asking to speak to this group, I promised not to make a pitch for my own computer company but to suggest simply the new opportunities available at low cost for maximizing textbook sales and profits. It happens that our company is the only one to have software already designed for this use and to have low-cost hardware ready for easy installation. If you'd like to talk about the system — its cost and management — I've a booth on Concourse C and will be available throughout the remainder of the convention. Without mentioning the name of the company, I'll just suggest that you look for a bright, red insignia over our display and consider a bright, red, and juicy — computer.

Thank you.

## HYPOTHETICAL SPEECH

Design a service of particular appeal to members of your class. Present a four- to five-minute speech selling that service by one of the rhetorical structures suggested in this chapter. Audience response to these sales speeches can be measured by mock-purchases of the service itself or of corporate stock.

## CRITIQUE FORM

Find an opportunity to observe a sales speech. Evaluate the speaker's effectiveness by completing the following form:

---

*Sales Speech*

Critic: _____

Date of speech: _____    Place: _____

Occasion: _____    Speaker: _____

Subject: _____

1. Summarize the event's context (i.e., audience profile, environmental variables):

2. Outline the sales speech and characterize its style:

3. Time of delivery in minutes: _____

4. Evaluate the communication merits and demerits of this sales speech. Assess its persuasive appeal.

# 19

# Demonstration Speech

DEFINITION

A demonstration speech is designed to show or to illustrate a product, process, or procedure. Its communication impact depends as much upon action as words, and real success demands a memorable combination of both modes. The rhetorical purpose of a demonstration may be to sell or to explain, linking its function to two other speech types discussed in these latter chapters. What makes a demonstration distinctive is not its aim but its method. Demonstrations pose special problems of delivery for the speaker and promise special rewards for an audience, when well done.

Speeches of demonstration are appropriate to many business settings. They can be used effectively for industrial training and employee orientation. They are indispensible to trade shows and sales conventions. Demonstration may be the best speech approach to a televised news release of new product information or innovative service design. In any setting, the decision whether or not to demonstrate depends on affirmative answers to the following questions:

1. Is the product, process, or procedure more likely to be remembered by its demonstration than by a verbal report with graphics?
2. Can a reliable, authentic demonstration be accommodated within the facilities, time, and space constraints of an occasion?
3. Does the speaker possess the required expertise to demonstrate the product, process, or procedure with authority?

If the answer to any of these questions is negative or in doubt, another speech approach should be considered. However, yes-answers to all three questions confirm a speaker's decision to demonstrate.

## SPEAKER

A speaker on this occasion is both teacher and actor. He or she must coordinate a narrative explanation in language with an ongoing physical (visual) demonstration. A good demonstration makes a procedure look simple to the audience, but no demonstration is simple for the speaker. Normal concentration must be split between talking and demonstrating. Normal control must be extended beyond oneself and one's voice to include myriad props, possible graphics, and table or floor space. Perhaps most difficult to gauge are the time requirements of a demonstration. One must know through careful practice exactly how many minutes it takes to *do* something as well as to *say* it. This means one must be able to control the speech environment. For example, a demonstration that takes ten minutes in one's own laboratory with familiar facilities may take much longer in the unfamiliar setting of a press room equipped with a simple table and an extension cord.

The relationship between language and action in a speech of demonstration is critical to success. As a general rule, a verbal summary should *precede* demonstration and then a detailed explanation should *accompany* demonstration. It is much less memorable for an audience to see a demonstration first and then hear description. Prior explanation sets up an anticipation for the audience of key operations to watch, and a step-by-step narrative during the visual event reinforces memory.

In any speech, good eye contact between speaker and audience pays communication dividends. In a demonstration, eye contact is essential. Unfortunately, it is difficult to maintain. Without eye contact, a speaker cannot assess how an audience is following the action, whether he or she is moving too quickly or slowly, and if all members of the audience can see and hear the presentation. A speaker's best delivery of a demonstration demands his or her alternating focus between the audience and the object being demonstrated. This means that neither notes nor manuscript can be used. At most, a demonstrator may rely on a brief outline reminding him or her of an operational sequence.

There is nothing more embarrassing for a speaker than coming to a critical moment in a demonstration and finding that a piece of equipment is missing or malfunctioning. A speaker should check out all equipment and facilities prior to a demonstration and test any operation that could possibly malfunction. Be sure to check lighting and sound for all positions of the demonstration. Do not rely on others to make a final check.

## AUDIENCE

The audience for a speech of demonstration is presumed to be interested in, or in need of, this special presentation. Demonstrations are best suited to audiences who will actually use a product or who will be expected to follow a procedure. When this need-to-know condition is met, a speaker may anticipate an eager and attentive audience.

We have said that no speech audience depends solely on aural perception: they are not simply listeners. The visual aspect of speech perception is on no occasion more dominant than in a demonstration. Audience members for this type of speech are viewers first and listeners second. They are, by implication, participants in the action, as each member of the audience puts himself or herself in the position of the demonstrator and tries to master the sequence of an operation.

While the product, process, or procedure of a demonstration is familiar to the speaker, he or she must remember that it is new to the audience. Viewers must be able to see, understand, and remember each step of a procedure. If a speaker watches carefully, audiences will give cues to their understanding. Viewers move about, nod, express confusion, and exclaim surprise in myriad ways both visible and audible to the speaker. When time allows, a demonstration can benefit from inviting questions from the audience during or after the event.

In many business situations, a viewer-listener is expected to know a process or procedure after one demonstration. Thus, a good speaker will assist the audience's memory with devices for remembering the sequence of steps in a procedure (e.g., by rhymes or acrostic codes). Remember that audience members for a demonstration are students, implied apprentices of the trade or operation being demonstrated.

## TEXT

The text (language, style, and structure) of a demonstration must be carefully worked out in advance of the occasion. Demonstrations may *look* casual and spontaneous, but good examples have been carefully organized on both the visual and verbal levels. The vocabulary of a demonstration speech should be as simple and precise as possible. The style, for most occasions, should be conversational and should invite audience response. The structure for all demonstrations must be sequential.

The verbal text for a speech of demonstration serves two functions — to announce and to explain. A speaker introduces the operation and narrates its demonstration. In fulfilling these two functions, the text is akin to a recipe that lists all ingredients and then explains a procedure through step-by-step instructions. A demonstration text begins with an introduction of the product, process, or procedure. Then, a catalog of necessary materials and facilities is listed and displayed. *Before* beginning the actual demonstration, a preview of the sequence should be given with special note of highlights. *As* the demonstration proceeds, the necessary sequence of steps should be underscored. *After* the demonstration, a review is helpful, with an explanation of any special problems or alternative operations not included in the demonstration. Again, a time for audience questions is useful for most speeches of demonstration.

## SUGGESTED FORMAT

1. Introduce the product, process, or procedure.
2. Display the required materials, ingredients, or facilities.
3. Preview the sequence of operational steps.
4. Demonstrate the product, process, or procedure with running narration.
5. Review the process and answer questions.

## SAMPLE SPEECH

Here is the transcript of a demonstration conducted by Charles Wright, chief electrical engineer for Pro-Tronics. He is demonstrating the advantages of proximity controls as opposed to photoelectric controls for an industrial operation at a paint plant. The manufacturing problem is to find a reliable way to automate putting lids on full paint cans. In the past, the step was accomplished at this plant by light sensitive photoelectric controls. Unhappy with this method, the management has contracted Pro-Tronics to install a better control system. This demonstration took place in the paint plant for an audience of fifteen to twenty managers and workers.

Okay, if you'll line up on both sides of the conveyor, everybody should be able to see. Please move right up to the conveyor. There should be enough room so that nobody has to stand behind somebody else.

As you know, the present system for releasing can lids is *this* photoelectric control. When a paint can passes under the photocell, the changed light conditions trigger the release and the lid press is activated. There are two problems with the system. First, the photoelectric controls have to be kept in constant adjustment and, when out of adjustment, can react to changes in room lighting and other unintended signals. Second, as you discovered with last week's costly accident, certain white paints reflect light in such a way that the photocell is not activated as it should be. The full paint can passes under the control without detection and havoc breaks loose at the end of the line. Let me demonstrate:

[A prearranged series of paint cans is set in motion to demonstrate the problem of the special white that does not activate the control.]

Now, if you'll move over to *this* conveyor, I'll show you the advantage of a proximity system. This control, attached at the side rather than the top of the conveyor, detects any paint can by its distance, not light. Let me demonstrate.

> [An identical prearranged series of paint cans is set in motion to demonstrate the efficiency of the proximity control.]
>
> Obviously, the kind of paint is of no consequence to this system. Lighting conditions do not alter efficiency. No control adjustments are required for various sized cans. An additional advantage of this system is its easy mounting. Without the photocell mounted above, the lid press will also be easier to repair.
>
> Proximity controls should solve all of the problems you've encountered with the photoelectric system at no greater cost. Now, what questions do you have?

## HYPOTHETICAL SPEECH

Choose a product or procedure to demonstrate in class with a ten-minute speech. The demonstration must include materials.

## CRITIQUE FORM

Find an opportunity to observe a demonstration speech. Evaluate the speaker's effectiveness by completing the following form:

---

*Demonstration Speech*

Critic: _____

Date of speech: _____     Place: _____

Occasion: _____     Speaker: _____

Subject: _____

1. Summarize the event's context (i.e., audience profile, environmental variables):

2. Outline the demonstration speech and summarize the relationship between verbal and visual communication:

3. Time of delivery in minutes: _____

4. Evaluate the communication merits and demerits of this demonstration speech. Assess its effectiveness in terms of increasing understanding of a product, process, or procedure.

# 20

# Speech of Explanation

## DEFINITION

"Explanation" is a generic term covering a number of different speech settings. The primary purpose of any speech of explanation is not to persuade but to inform. Explanations are required in business to announce policy, to explicate philosophy, to answer questions, and to defend vested interests and corporate positions. Explanations are offered in both congenial and adversary circumstances before audiences that are sometimes friendly and sometimes antagonistic to the speaker. A good explanation can increase understanding, simplify complexity, and reduce tension. Effective explanation can build a foundation for later persuasion.

## SPEAKER

To deliver a successful speech of explanation, one must (1) know a subject thoroughly and (2) anticipate the audience's prior knowledge and predisposition toward the subject. Preparation for this type of speech begins with a speaker listing the specific items of information or the training objectives that an audience should learn by the end of the speech. Then one must calculate where an audience is likely to begin the educational process. Composition demands finding the most efficient structure for moving the audience from their state of prior knowledge to the desired state of acquired knowledge.

All choices of composition and delivery must be made to enhance precision from the speaker's viewpoint and clarity from the listener's perspective. Unlike a demonstration that relies primarily on visual communication, a speech of explanation relies primarily on verbal skills. A speaker's control of language, style, and structure is indispensible to successful explanation. Because the speech context for an explanation implies greater knowledge on the speaker's part than on the listener's, one must be especially careful to avoid a vocabulary or a tone of voice that is condescending toward, or patronizing of, the audience.

## AUDIENCE

The degree of audience attentiveness to an explanation depends upon the clarity of a speaker's presentation *and* upon the attitudes, beliefs, opinions, and prior information possessed by each listener. In a situation where the audience *demands* some explanation, the adversary relationship between speaker and listener may cause considerable resistance and possible distortion of the speaker's message on the part of an audience. This resistance must be countered by the speaker's feeling and thinking *into* the listener's point of view and anticipating an audience's concerns. Understanding must begin on the speaker's part as he or she takes on a listener's perspective. Only after the audience feels assured that their viewpoints and vested interests have been taken into account are they likely to work at understanding the speaker's position.

Implicit in any speech of explanation is an assumed question on the listener's part. Unless someone asks a question, explicitly or implicitly, no explanation is required. A speaker's task in relating well to the audience is finding out exactly what question is being asked. If the listener wants to know "why," he or she will not be satisfied with the answer to "how"; if the question is "when," a "where" answer will not suffice. When the answer matches the question, and when the explanation is both sensible and complete, this type of speech is likely to succeed. Total agreement between speaker and listener may not result, but better understanding will be achieved. And that is the aim of an explanation.

## TEXT

The text of a speech of explanation must address the questions uppermost in an audience's mind. Language must be forthright, and a structure must be found to aid understanding in the most direct way. Many patterns of organization exist for speeches of explanation. When the problem to be explained is obvious to both speaker and audience, the best speech approach may be a simple *problem-solution* or *question-answer* structure. When the problem itself is less clear, a *cause and effect* analysis may be required. To clarify the context of a problem or its solution, a *chronological* explanation or a deductive argument illustrating the particular outcome of a broad policy (i.e., a *general to specific* rhetorical structure) may be helpful. In circumstances when a problem or an explanation is especially complicated, understanding may be aided by the use of an *analogy* or a detailed *comparison and contrast* analysis. A speaker's choice of the most useful structure assumes that he or she knows the audience's vested interests and prior knowledge and knows exactly what added information is necessary to their understanding of a given issue.

## SUGGESTED FORMATS

Here are summarized six typical approaches to a speech of explanation.

### Suggested Format 1: Question-Answer

1. State the question or problem and define its terms.
2. Explain the answer or solution with acknowledgment of the speaker's viewpoint.
3. Defend the answer or solution with logical discussion and documented evidence.

### Suggested Format 2: Cause and Effect

1. Summarize the status quo and define its problem.
2. Work backward through time to discover probable causes of the current dilemma. Test each probability to prove the logic of a causal link.

Or

1. Summarize the status quo.
2. Work forward through time to predict the probable consequences of a current course of action. Be sure to illustrate all logical steps (causal links) in the predictive argument.

## Suggested Format 3: Chronological

1. Summarize the status quo and define its problem.
2. Fill in a time line of past circumstances (not necessarily causal) that shed light on a current dilemma.
3. Explain the definition or understanding of a problem as altered by this temporal background.

## Suggested Format 4: General to Specific

1. State a general policy or philosophy and define its terms.
2. Trace the specific applications or ramifications of that general position in particular procedures or actions.
3. Explain the relationship between a given policy and a specific procedure required to understand both.

## Suggested Format 5: Analogy

1. Outline a familiar object or operation.
2. Define and explain a new or unfamiliar object or operation by comparing its salient features with those of the familiar item. (The logical validity of an analogy depends upon a point-by-point comparison between two unlike things.)

## Suggested Format 6: Comparison and Contrast

1. Introduce a series of related objects or operations.
2. Illustrate the definitive characteristics of each item as specifically as possible.
3. Analyze the similarities and differences among related items.
4. Evaluate the comparative qualities of the object of explanation.

## SAMPLE SPEECH

Maggie Schaffer is director of public relations for an American car manufacturer. Here is her brief speech explaining the procedure for a national recall. Notice that the implied questions being answered are "why" the recall and, more importantly, "how" to implement the recall. The speech was made as part of a press conference.

> Ladies and gentlemen, the ____(company)____ hereby notifies owners of our models __(name)__ and __(name)__ subcompact cars that we are recalling all front-wheel drive 1982 cars to be inspected for possibly damaged wheel bearings.
>
> Our quality control department has discovered that the bearings on the front wheels of these particular automobiles may have been damaged while in manufacture. The defective bearings could cause front-wheel and axle-shaft problems, although no injuries, accidents, or complaints have been reported of this possible defect.
>
> Owners of the 1982 models __(name)__ or __(name)__ subcompact cars with front-wheel drive should follow this procedure. Call your local ____(company)____ dealer and make an appointment to have the front wheel bearings inspected. The inspection of the bearings takes no longer than twenty minutes to complete. If the bearings are found to be damaged, repair can be done in one to two hours at no cost to the owner.
>
> The owner will be asked to fill out a short form at the dealer's office. This form notifies our company that the owner has responded to the recall and indicates whether repair work was necessary.
>
> Thank you.

## HYPOTHETICAL SPEECH

In a ten-minute speech, explain the capitalist system to a class of third graders.

## CRITIQUE FORM

Find an opportunity to observe a speech of explanation. Evaluate the speaker's effectiveness by completing the following form:

*Speech of Explanation*

Critic: _____

Date of speech: _____    Place: _____

Occasion: _____    Speaker: _____

Subject: _____

1. Summarize the event's context (i.e., audience profile, environmental variables):

2. Outline the speech's structure, characterize its style, and identify the question being answered:

3. Time of delivery in minutes: _____

4. Evaluate the communication merits and demerits of this speech of explanation.

# 21

# Motivational Speech

## DEFINITION

A motivational speech aims to create positive change in a listener's attitude or behavior. Depending upon the context, this desired change may be from a negative predisposition to a positive one or from a position of mild interest to real commitment. A motivational speech does not sell a product or a service; it sells an *attitude*. Fundamentally, a speech of motivation aims to change a listener's view of himself or herself within a given business context.

## SPEAKER

As with any other speech assignment, a motivational speaker must operate from a set of specific objectives. He or she must know precisely the targeted attitude change in an audience. Like the results of a sales speech, the results of a successful motivational speech will be measurable in visible behavior change. A speaker dare not leave this process of change to chance or define it in vague generalities. One must calculate the existing attitudes of an audience, outline the target attitudes, and design a step-by-step strategy for positive change.

With most motivational speeches, a speaker has no sales brochure or object of demonstration to enhance the verbal presentation. The speaker himself or herself *represents* the attitude to be sold. A successful speech of motivation depends entirely upon the speaker's own presence as a tangible model of the desired attitude. Where the speaker's viewpoint or commitment are not clear and credible, no sale can be made. It is not enough, though, that the speaker be convinced of a given perspective. He or she must persuade the audience of their need to change — to adopt a similar attitude to the speaker's. In addition to high credibility, a speaker must establish rapport with the audience so that they may work together toward a common good rather than feeling any adversary resistance.

The common ground shared by a speaker and an audience in most business settings is defined by corporate objectives. The motivation for individual attitude change is one's desire to fulfill, or to fulfill more completely, a given corporate objective (e.g., product excellence, profitability, or service reputation). Successful motivation in the business context *assumes* a shared loyalty between speaker and listener to stated corporate objectives.

## AUDIENCE

Audiences for motivational speeches divide into two major camps — those individuals willing and eager to change and those hesitant or resistant to change. A different speech (and, perhaps, a different speaker) is required by these audiences. Listeners who are eager to change (e.g., who want to sell more) need to be told *how*. Listeners who are resistant to change (e.g., who prefer the status quo) need to be told *why*. An answer to the why-question will seem unnecessary to the first audience. An answer to the how-question will seem presumptuous and bullying to the second audience.

Human beings, comfortable in our work habits and routine attitudes, may find change threatening and difficult to handle. When such a threat exists in the predisposition of an audience, the speaker must address directly the listener's insecurity. Attitude change involves taking risks, stepping into an unfamiliar territory. For a motivational speech to achieve real changes of attitude and behavior in the audience, a corporate context must provide enough security to encourage risk taking. Motivation for attitudinal or behavioral change is usually linked to specific inducements or rewards.

## TEXT

We said that some audiences for this kind of speech are interested primarily in how to change and others are concerned with why change is necessary. The text of a good motivational speech addresses both questions, though varying the emphasis between these two variables depending on the predisposition of a given audience. Simply put, a listener will not change until he or she understands the need to change (why) and the process of change (how). Both conditions are necessary, and their sequence (first why and then how) is essential.

An answer to the question *why* change is necessary may be the proven insufficiency of a current attitude or behavior—an essentially negative argument. Or the answer may be a positive argument based on the comparative advantages of a changed attitude or behavior over the benefits of the status quo. The *how* question is often more difficult to answer. Although no formula can be taught to achieve attitude change, one rhetorical guideline should be learned. That is, attitude change is a process requiring many steps, not one leap. Old habits and patterns of thought must be broken one by one and replaced individually with the building blocks of a new or altered attitude. This process of mental and emotional construction cannot be accomplished by decree or by a simple act of the will. It can only be achieved by a usually painstaking deconstruction of an existing attitude and the slow construction of a new viewpoint. A good speaker understands the process and can offer an architectural design, as it were, for guiding an orderly change.

(An interesting debate exists as to whether attitude change must predate behavioral change or whether a changed behavior elicits a changed attitude. It would not serve our purpose here to join the debate except to say that behavior and attitude are integrally connected, and the boundaries of each overlap the other).

The text of a good motivational speech, then, must answer the questions "why" and "how." It must guide the listener through an orderly process of change—a change worth the effort required to achieve and a change represented positively in the speaker's own viewpoint and behavior.

## SUGGESTED FORMAT

1. Define the target attitude, viewpoint, or behavior.
2. Answer the question "why" change is necessary by arguing *against* the defects in the status quo or *for* the benefits of the proposed change. The rationale for personal changes of attitude or behavior must be justified by adherence to stated corporate objectives.
3. Describe "how" this desired change can be accomplished by suggesting specific steps in an orderly sequence.
4. Assure the audience of the advantages in changing, and outline any specific inducements for change within the corporate context.

## SAMPLE SPEECH

Here is the transcript of a motivational speech in which a representative of a local steel worker's union tries to persuade his members to adopt a contract offer. The question embedded in this speech is "Why should we, the workers, make concessions to management?" To motivate a changed attitude and to elicit an affirmative vote, the speaker must answer that why-question.

---

Here's the proposal. Management will meet all other demands IF we concede three of our paid holidays and accept an annual pay increase of two percent. All right. All right. I know it's not what we want, but let's not reject it without giving the thing a chance. Just listen.

We all know the economy has been lousy, and a lot of things have hit steel especially hard. Many other companies have had to shut down, and we're trying with this contract to avoid the same fate.

In the present circumstances, it's in our best interest to cooperate with management, and let me tell you why. We didn't go into these negotiations with our eyes closed. We've made management back up their claims of financial hardship. For the first time ever in our years of negotiation with this company, the union has been permitted to do an independent audit. Do you hear me? We've seen the figures. The money just isn't there to give the pay increases we want. And we're not the only ones paying the fiddler. Management has frozen all future administrative hiring, planned to phase out twenty percent of desk jobs over the next year, and will take absolutely no pay increase (including stock and bonuses) in the next year.

Now, if we accept the contract as it is, we should all be working twelve months in the next year. We will be in a stronger position for future negotiations. If we reject the contract offer, there is NO GIVE. As I see it, a vote for the contract is a vote for your job. A vote against the contract is a vote against your own job. Think, and I urge you to vote yes.

---

## HYPOTHETICAL SPEECH

Deliver a 7-minute speech designed to change a specific predisposition in your classroom audience. Choose a topic (e.g., a political viewpoint or a personal value) about which you feel strongly and toward which you may anticipate some opposition from the audience. After the speech, discuss whether any attitude change actually occurred, or is likely to occur in the future, as the result of this presentation.

## CRITIQUE FORM

Find an opportunity to observe a motivational speech. Evaluate the speaker's effectiveness by completing the following form:

*Motivational Speech*

Critic: _____

Date of speech: _____  Place: _____

Occasion: _____  Speaker: _____

Subject: _____

1. Summarize the event's context (i.e., audience profile, environmental variables):

2. Outline the speech's structure, characterize its style, and identify the motivating rationale:

3. Time of delivery in minutes: _____

4. Evaluate the communication merits and demerits of this motivational speech.

# 22

# Verbal Report

## DEFINITION

A verbal report is a special kind of informative speech called for specifically by an audience or by a formal schedule of corporate accountability. As its name suggests, the verbal report is a transitional mode of communication between a written document and a speech event. Often, this type of speech is read by the speaker and, frequently, printed copies are made available to the audience before or after delivery. The structure of a verbal report also bears resemblance to written discourse with its linear sequence of headings.

Verbal reports are appropriate to many business settings, most of them formal. The reading of minutes at a committee or board meeting represents a verbal report. The presentation of financial statements, treasurer's reports, research findings, committee deliberations, and task force recommendations are some of the more common instances of this report type. Common to all is a sense of specific accountability, on the speaker's part, to the audience. Verbal reports are made in response to dated assignments. The term "report" carries connotations of subject *and* audience: a speaker must report *something* to *someone* (and usually by a certain deadline).

## ΞAKER

One who delivers a verbal report acknowledges his or her accountability to an audience by specifying the report's assignment and never wavering from its mandates in the speech's development. This speaker aims to divert attention away from himself or herself, away from the audience's vested interests, away from a particular commercial context and *toward* the clear and concise presentation of information. The credibility of a verbal report depends upon an audience's perception of a factually based and empirically verified account. A good reporter offers facts before conclusions and data before interpretation. A good verbal report ought not to depend for its validity upon a speaker's viewpoint but upon the clarity of the data themselves and the logical strength of their presentation. The speaker must present all information in a sensible sequence, and he or she must make clear the rational steps in a logical analysis.

Because many verbal reports in business rely upon numbers, percentages, and fractions for their data base, a speaker does well to incorporate visual aids into a presentation — charts, tables, and graphs. If well designed and professionally produced, these can clarify and make memorable information otherwise difficult to communicate verbally. The graphics enhance the oral presentation with visual support.

## AUDIENCE

The audience for a verbal report sets the agenda, as it were. Members of the audience usually come to an event knowing the speaker's assignment and looking for specific information in response to that assignment. For instance, an audience holds the speaker formally accountable for complete minutes or accurate financial reporting.

The typical listener to a verbal report brings with him or her certain readerly expectations. We said that this type of assignment places the speaker in a middle ground between written and verbal discourse. The same is true of an audience's perceptual framework. The formality of a report's commercial context imposes categories of expectation upon a text. The audience comes prepared with a mental checklist of items that should be covered in a competent report. This checklist is overlaid upon the speech as an equivalent of the reader's scanning mechanism. Most often, verbal reports are also published in print form, and the audience expects a linear sequencing of information akin to a reading experience.

## TEXT

Texts for verbal reports vary widely and are usually prescribed by the occasion. Specific formulas exist for recording minutes, accounting for financial figures, and reporting research findings.[1] Any generic outline simply serves to reinforce the mandate that all

---

[1] For a complete discussion of business report formats, see the author's *The Business Report: Writer, Reader, and Text* (Englewood Cliffs, New Jersey: Prentice-Hall, Inc., 1983).

report types must proceed from facts to interpretation, data to analysis, or description to evaluation. A verbal report for which no prescribed format exists may proceed in this general sequence. First, the report's thesis or research question is explicated. Second, a methodology for gathering and interpreting data is explained and defended. Third, data are presented in words and figures. Fourth, these data are analyzed, and their statistical significance is discussed. Fifth, conclusions are drawn or a summary presented. Sixth, recommendations are offered. Again, the necessary sequence of this rhetorical structure moves from description to evaluation (e.g., recommendations *cannot* be presented before data and analysis).

## SUGGESTED FORMAT

1. Explicate the thesis or research question.
2. Explain the method of data collection and interpretation.
3. Present the data.
4. Analyze the data.
5. Present a summary and draw conclusions.
6. Offer recommendations.

## SAMPLE SPEECH

Here is a verbal report of quarterly income presented by the president and chief operating officer of ACP Corporation to a meeting of the board of directors. Board members received three documents that were printed supplements to the speech: (1) Condensed Statements of Income, (2) Condensed Balance Sheets, and (3) Condensed Statements of Changes in Financial Position. After acceptance by the board, this same information was published in print form and distributed to corporate shareholders.

Fourth Quarter Report of ACP Corporation
December 31, 1982

*Overview*

ACP achieved fourth quarter earnings for the period ending December 31, 1982 of $.43 per share, a 21 percent increase from $.35 per share for the fourth quarter of 1981. Net income increased to $6,283,000, from $5,220,000, a 20 percent increase.

Operating revenue for the fourth quarter increased 16 percent to $158.9 million from $135.6 million a year ago. For the year 1982, earnings per share were at a new high of $1.42 per share, a 22 percent increase from $1.17 per share in 1981. Net income increased to $21.1 million from $17.5 million, a 21 percent increase. Operating revenue for the year increased 18 percent to $589 million, from $499 million a year ago.

APC had a record year of revenue growth. At the end of 1982, annualized revenue from all products and services combined was $629.7 million, representing an increase of $100.2 million, or 19 percent over the beginning of the year. Inflation-related growth in revenue was less in 1982 than in previous years.

### Dividends

We, the Board of Directors, declared a new quarterly dividend rate of $.28 per share compared with dividends of $.23 per share paid on January 31, 1982, a 20 percent increase. Dividends paid in 1982 were $1.00 per share, and the annual indicated dividend for 1983 is $1.15 per share. The dividend increase represents the twenty-second increase since 1968.

## HYPOTHETICAL SPEECH

Give a verbal report announcing a drop in per share earnings for one year in a fictitious corporation. Show, by comparing the figure with per share earnings of the previous ten years, why the current drop is *not* a cause for undue concern on the part of stockholders. For this assignment, you will need to invent the corporate name and supporting financial figures.

## CRITIQUE FORM

Find an opportunity to observe a verbal report. Evaluate the speaker's effectiveness by completing the following form:

*Verbal Report*

Critic: _____

Date of speech: _____     Place: _____

Occasion: _____     Speaker: _____

Subject: _____

1. Summarize the event's context (i.e., audience profile, environmental variables):

2. Outline the speech's structure, characterize its style, and identify any graphic aids used:

3. Time of delivery in minutes: _____

4. Evaluate the communication merits and demerits of this verbal report.

# Appendix

# Strategies for Continued Study

It is customary for a text of this kind to include a bibliography or list of suggested readings for further study. The drawback of concluding this text with such a list is the implication, despite disclaimers, that one *can* compile a comprehensive bibliography — or even a representative one. The fact is that there are scores of valuable books and hundreds of insightful articles written on aspects of business speaking that have been published in just the past ten years. Any bibliography would soon be dated by its exclusion of current resources. Thus, instead of this traditional approach, here are four strategies that you may follow to supplement and continue your study of business speaking.

## IN-HOUSE CRITICISM

The first (and best) resource for continued study are the files of speeches made every day as part of a given business operation. As managers acknowledge the importance of communication skills at every level of the corporate enterprise, many companies have started in-house educational programs to improve the public speaking skills of employees.

One facet of these programs is a study group composed of senior and junior employees who exchange descriptive criticism of one another's speeches. These in-house study programs, if well structured and directed, can provide a support group for the continuing development of business speakers, no matter how much experience one may have.

## BOOKS AND PAMPHLETS

A second resource for further study are books and pamphlets on business communication and public speaking. There is a long and rich history of such texts dating back to the early part of this century. Although the formats and language of the earliest texts may now seem quite dated, even these can prove fascinating reading as one analyzes changing perceptions and definitions of business communication.

To find useful books in your university, college, or public library, look in the subject index of the card catalog. Ordinarily, books on business speaking can be found under one of the following Library of Congress subject headings:

After dinner speeches
Business education
Business ethics
Business literature
Collaborative authorship
Commercial statistics
Communication in management
Creative ability in business
Extemporaneous speaking
Ghostwriting
Introduction of speakers
Lectures and lecturing
Mass media and business
Oral communication
Orations
Speech acts
Speech errors
Speech perception
Toasts

## JOURNALS

Professional and academic journals are invaluable resources for any in-depth study of business communication. These are easy to find if you know how to start the search.

Begin in the reference room with the *Business Periodical Index*. This annual reference book indexes the contents of some 250 journals and magazines devoted to business, economics, public relations, and management. At the front of the book, you will find the titles (and addresses) of all these periodicals listed in alphabetical order. To find articles in the *BPI* on business speech, look under the following headings:

Business communication
Communication
Communication in management
Employee communication
Public speaking
Speech

Note the title of the article, the date of the journal, and the page numbers. Then find the back issue either among bound periodicals or microtexts.

An especially valuable periodical for the student of public speaking is *Vital Speeches of the Day*, a twice-monthly publication of complete transcripts of current speeches.

## NEWSPAPERS

A fourth helpful resource for continued study are the business sections of newspapers. A careful search of these can provide a wealth of specific examples of how business communication works day to day. Begin this approach to research by referring to two annual indexes: *The New York Times Index* and *The Wall Street Journal Index*. Look up articles under the same subject headings as in the *BPI*.